Dedication

To my sister Oreathel who "mothered" me
when I was a child. She has been
a helpful resource person about events
in our early lives.

And to my dear wife, Louise, who has
been such an asset to my life,
my ministry, and my writings.

To Roy & Marilyn,
God bless you, dear
friends, and fill your
life with True riches!
L. A. Kennedy

Contents

Introduction

If the title of my book (taken from 2 Corinthians 4:7) seems strange, consider this. An earthen vessel is not a rare piece of art fashioned from gold, silver, or bronze. It is a simple vessel formed from humble clay. It is God's "treasure" in it that makes the difference.

My hope is that this book will give you a greater appreciation of common people and the glory of the commonplace. There are wonders in all these if we only have eyes to see. Thomas Gray saw it in "Elegy Written In A Country Churchyard." There he extolled "The short and simple annals of the poor." Robert Burns saw it in "The Cotter's Saturday Night."

This book is factual, humorous, and inspirational. The people and events are real. Each has made a lasting impression upon my life. While the passing years have made it near impossible to reproduce much of the dialogue verbatim, the sense of what was said is accurate.

The account is autobiographical, covering the long span of my lifetime. My early years were spent in cotton fields and farm work. Since age 20, I have served 52 years in the gospel ministry. During 22 of those years, I also taught in a Baptist college. By the grace of God I have enjoyed a full and interesting life. But it has not come by my goodness, wisdom, nor power. I am indeed an earthen vessel.

This book is more than the story of my life and family. It contains stories of churches where I have preached. It introduces you to friends, college colleagues, and interesting acquaintances. You may even find yourself in it.

One who has preached for more than half a century has seen many humorous incidents. That renowned pastor-counselor R. Lofton Hudson observed:

> You have to keep up your laugh life as well as your love life. I cannot imagine anything much worse in this life for someone in my family to say

1

after I died, "Well, I'm sorry he had to die, but he was awfully boring the last years of his life." Or, "We'll miss him, but he got to where he wasn't any fun to be around."[1]

Humor is healthful. The Bible says, "A cheerful heart is a good medicine...."[2] I laughed often, and I hope you will laugh with me.

This book is inspirational. James cautioned us against despising the poor.[3] There is so much we may learn from poor, ordinary people. Many of them are far more generous and helpful than most affluent people. They tend to be more hospitable. Often they exemplify great faith, even in suffering, losses, and injustices.

In this book I will introduce you to many common people, churches, and institutions with an uncommon commitment. Remembering them, I have shed tears of appreciation and gratitude. I hope you will too. After 52 years of preaching, like Shakespeare I sometimes see "sermons in stones."

Is it a waste of time to minister among the poor and uneducated? Jesus certainly did not think so. Their souls were as precious to him as the souls of the greatest and most learned of men.

I have had no desire to engage in religious competition with my brother ministers nor to become known as a "go-getter." Building large budgets and church edifaces never appealed to me as such.

While I have often failed, the yearning of my heart and aim of my life have been to magnify Christ in a spiritual ministry. From first to last I long to be a Christocentric man—with Christ at the center and circumference of my whole life. I wanted to be pastor, not of large churches but spiritual churches. Such congregations are missionary in outreach and offer an unconditional acceptance of others.

It isn't that my life has been any harder or fuller than many others. One difference may be that God has blessed me with greater powers of retention than most others have.

To a large extent reading is the unlocking of memory. I hope that, as you read these pages, you will be reminded of many of your own experiences and insights.

I hope you will develop a deeper appreciation for your own roots and for the many simple people who have helped make you into what you are. "Look to the rock from which you were cut and to the quarry from which you were hewn..."[4]

But keep growing and never become a captive of the past.

Chapter 1

From Cotton Patch To College Professor

Two of my Appalachian students, Gerald and Delbert, walked slowly into my office at Campbellsville College (now University). Both were enrolled in a remedial course that I taught for those whose skills were too low for regular Freshman English.

"Good morning," I greeted them. "How can I help you?"

"We've come to tell you goodbye," Gerald informed me. "We're dropping out and going back home."

"Why?" I implored.

"Well, in the little schools we attended in the mountains we didn't get enough preparation for college. We'll just have to go back and work in the coal mines as our families have always done."

"Don't leave now," I begged them. "Stay at least this semester and really try hard. I believe I can help you acquire the basic English skills you need to succeed in college. That's what our class is for."

"But, Mr. Kennedy, you don't understand. We're both from poor families. We attended little one-room schools in the mountains. You've come from a privileged family and had things better than us."

"Please sit down a few minutes," I urged, "while I share something that may surprise you."

Then I told them about my uneducated parents, my labors in the cotton fields of Tennessee and Texas, the early death of my father in 1937 leaving me at 12 the older son of our family.

"But as I pulled my heavy sacks of cotton down the long cotton rows, back bent and face toward the ground, I prayed that God would take me out of the fields, help me get an education, and give me opportunity to share his

5

goodness and truth with other people. I claimed his promise, 'If thou canst believe, all things are possible to him that believeth.'[5]

"He answered my prayers, took me out of the cotton patch, and has given me one of the most exciting of lives. You know me as a preacher and college professor, but my early life was just as discouraging and hard as yours. Pray, believe, and work hard, and he will keep you out of the coal mines and give you a fuller life, too."

Not convinced, Delbert went on back to Pike County. I never heard from him again. Gerald followed my advice (and his dreams). A few years later he graduated with honors from our college. Then he earned the master's and doctor's degrees from other schools. He has been a successful educator in East Tennessee.

I told Gerald and Delbert that any young person who wants it badly enough can have a great and successful life. Of course, this does not necessarily involve becoming rich nor gaining fame or recognition as a celebrity. It may not involve freedom from disappointments, problems, or suffering. Rather, the truly successful life is one effectively spent in glorifying God and ministering to one's fellowman. Jesus stressed, "The greatest among you will be your servant."[6]

Some say I was almost born in a cotton field near Marston, Missouri. My mother always worked side-by-side with Daddy and the family in the fields. But on this day, October 17, 1924, she was home.

The doctor who delivered me was nearly drunk, so he thought it funny to jumble up my vital statistics. Mother's maiden name was Lubie White. He recorded it as Lubie Black. Then he recorded my sex as female and my name as Laurel Dean! Years later, when I applied for a birth certificate, I found out what had happened.

During World War II, I worked as a chemical operator at Oak Ridge, Tennessee. The F.B.I. hassled me to get an accurate birth certificate, but I could not. It was not until 1975, as I prepared to lead a tour to Israel, that I finally succeeded, through the assistance of my U.S. congressman.

Over the years I have been teased a great deal about my name, L. D. (It seems that in 1924 it was rather common for parents to give an initials-only name to their sons.) Car rental agencies sometimes make up a name for me, maintaining that their computer form will not take initials. On business and legal applications I am often required to insert (i.o.) after each initial. So some have called me Leo Deo.

After I was born my little sister Oreathel hid behind the door and pouted because she would be the baby no longer. To appease her, my mother urged, "Come on out and see him. He can be your baby, and I'll let you name him."

Oreathel looked about the room until her eyes fell upon a glass doorknob that she especially liked. So she turned to Mother and said, "We'll call him Doorknob."

Perhaps that would not have been an unfitting name because I was born in the "show-me" state and have more than once been accused of being hardheaded!

L.D. in yard at Obion River
Elbow near Bogota

Oreathel, L.D. Genova at
Dawson Farm, Dotsonville, TX

Daddy at window of train car holding Delbert. L.D. below.

Chapter 2

Daddy Was A "Rolling Stone"

My father was Marcus D. Lafayette Kennedy, but everyone called him Fate. He was a hard-working farmer. Some years he made a sharecrop. But usually he and our family just worked as day laborers.

Wages then for farm work were unbelievably low. For this reason Daddy moved a lot, always trying to find more work, better pay, or a better house for us to live in.

Mamma, who disliked moving, called Daddy "a rolling stone." His rejoinder was that "a rolling stone never gathers any moss."

When I was a baby, our family left the flat "bootheel" country of Missouri. Our new "home" was a little shack on "the Elbow" of the Obion River near Bogota, Tennessee. Daddy enjoyed fishing in "the Elbow," for some huge catfish were caught in its deep swirling waters.

Sometime later we moved to a little community southwest of Bogota called Barbwire. My sister Oreathel, three and one-half years older than I, cared for me while Mother picked cotton.

"If anything happens, come to the window and wave this diaper," Mother told Oreathel. "Then I'll know you want me to come." Mother had told her that when I wet or soiled my diaper to take it off and clean me but not try to put it back on.

One day Oreathel must have grown tired of seeing me strut around in the nude, so she decided to diaper me herself. In so doing she ran the pin through the lower end of my foreskin, leaving a scar that I inquired about when I got older.

For two successive years the Obion and Mississippi rivers flooded Dad's crops at Barbwire, resulting in dread-

11

ful crop failures. Most of us were sick a lot with malaria, a common disease then carried by the blood-sucking mosquitoes of the river bottom country. Discouragement reigned.

A cousin, Arthur Gallaway, kept writing letters trying to persuade my parents and other relatives to move to the Panhandle section of West Texas where he lived. He emphasized that there was no malaria there and plenty of cotton to pick.

So in the fall of 1927 we crammed our essential belongings into the Model-T Fords of Uncle Dee White (Mother's brother) and Uncle Arthur Jones (Daddy's brother-in-law). It took about five days for the slow, heavily-loaded, Model-Ts to crawl over the rutted dirt and gravel roads to Dodsonville (now Dodson), Texas.

Along the way we spotted many vacant houses. Nightly we would spread our pallets and sleep in them, with permission from the owner if we could locate him.

My first remembrance took place at that time, when I was nearly three years old. At the end of one of the tiring days, we children rolled out of our tight quarters to explore our house for the night. With shouts of delight we saw that the yard was covered with white sand. Barefooted we ran and jumped into it. Then we screamed in pain when we encountered something new to us—sandburs.

After arriving at Arthur Gallaway's, we first stayed in a big tent at the edge of his cotton field. I enjoyed lying on my back, feeling and watching the red glow from the Texas sun shining through the canvas. Another memory is the smell of vanilla tea cakes my mother frequently baked. The enticing aroma filled the tent and even reached out to the cotton field.

Soon Daddy made a deal with Gene Dawson to share-crop for him the following year. Mr. Dawson let us move into his big one-room shack, with no partitions. Mother, especially, was happy to get out of the tent.

By age four I was allowed to go to the field with our family and pick cotton. Mamma sewed a strap on a little three-foot burlap "toe-sack," and I proudly became a cotton picker. My parents told me that I picked more than a bale of cotton the year I was five. At seven I got a seven-foot sack made of ducking and soon pulled one nine-foot long.

While the field work was hard for a child, I have many happy memories of family life in those days. At noonday when the Texas sun was bearing down, we would take shade under the cotton wagon and eat our simple lunch. As we rested there Daddy often delighted us children with humorous songs, such as "Froggie Went a-Courtin'," "The Old Maid," and "Crawdad Song."

I will never forget his "Laughing Song" that he did with his deep resonant voice. It caused us children to roll with delight. Sometimes he told us stories of great Bible characters. When Daddy entertained, the days didn't seem as long nor the work as hard.

Also, I will always be indebted to Oreathel as my "little mother" during my tender years. She loved me and watched over me faithfully. Moreover, she was a born storyteller with a vivid imagination. She made up her stories as she told them and always kept me in suspense about what was coming next. Once she even convinced me that Santa Claus would soon be coming through a large knothole in our pine wall!

Over the years Oreathel instilled in me a love for literature and for writing. It was an honor and joy to have her one semester as a student in my Creative Writing class at Campbellsville College. But she taught me more than I ever taught her.

Mamma's sister, Aunt Mirtie Millner, wrote sad letters about how their family in Tennessee were battling recurring bouts of malaria. So Daddy and Mamma sent them money to come on a train to Texas to live. We let them stay with us in our big one-room shack until they could get a place of their own.

Sleeping posed a bit of a problem since we had only two beds. Mamma, Daddy, and my little brother Delbert slept in one bed. Uncle Cleve, Aunt Mirtie, and their baby Marie, slept in the other bed. The rest of us children slept on pallets on the floor.

Food was rather scarce. One day Uncle Cleve shot a hawk, and Aunt Mirtie cooked it for us.

When we left the Dawson place, we moved to Dodsonville and lived for awhile in a train coach by the railroad track. Daddy and Uncle Cleve worked as section hands. The coach wasn't so bad. It had two big rooms, windows, and a door.

We children were fascinated by the long, earth-shaking trains that roared by us daily. I learned to count by counting the boxcars, often more than 200. We enjoyed waving at the conductor and other trainmen, and they would smile and wave back.

Our older sister, Genova, thrilled us when she read for us the names of distant states on the boxcars. When no train was coming we children walked the tracks to see who could go farthest without failing off. In the summertime this was quite a hot walk since all of us were barefooted. Always, wherever we lived, we found fun things to do.

While we stayed in some unusual places, we never ceased to be a loving and tightly-knit family. The type of roof over our heads could not alter the dignity, faith, and mutual respect that glowed within our hearts.

I do not now remember the name of the rail line that passed through Dodsonville. But I well remember one generous custom it had. At Christmastime during those depression years a train would pass slowly through our little village while trainmen tossed out to us waiting children candy and small gifts. These were the only presents some of the children got.

Chapter 3

Grandpa Was a Legend

My grandfather "Toob" Kennedy was a kind of legend in his day. He had a better-than-average education and had even taught school. Yet for weeks at a time his mind left him, probably from a blow on his head while working at a sawmill. (Doctors thought his injury had produced a tumor on the brain.)

When his mind was bad, he abused Grandma Bashebe, who was part Indian. Daddy said that on one occasion Grandpa caught Grandma and cut off her beautiful black hair with a butcher knife. She finally had to leave him and return to relatives at Trenton, Tennessee. When she left, he would not let her take the children with her. Fortunately, he never tried to injure any of them.

During his spells, Grandpa was thrown into jails and mental institutions but none could hold him for long. A tall huge man of about 300 pounds, he was so strong that several men had difficulty subduing him.

In one jail he set fire to the bedding. When the jailors came to extinguish the blaze, he overcame them and escaped. On another occasion he pried off the cell door of the jail at Lexington, Tennessee, without any tool.

While unafraid of strong men, Grandpa had a great fear of what he call microbes. Once he burned a house down to get rid of bed bugs. Another time he chopped up his featherbed and scattered all the feathers.

When his mind went bad, he would gather up his two boys (Daddy and Brownlow) and three of his girls (Mollie, Sarah and Lucy) and set out on foot from place to place. They would raid gardens and hen houses or beg for food as they went through communities.

At night they slept in a barn or vacant house or on the ground under whatever shelter they could find. Daddy said

15

he remembered waking up a few times with his clothes frozen to the ground. Grandpa had let the fire go out.

While visiting in Tennessee, Cousin Will Kennedy told Grandpa what a great place the Indian Territory was, begging him to go back with him. It sounded like an exciting adventure to Grandpa. So he loaded his children into Will's covered wagon. With high hopes they started to the Indian Territory.

By the time they reached the Mississippi River a serious argument erupted between the two men. Cousin Will headed west in his wagon, leaving them behind. Grandpa hired a man with a small skiff to take him and his family across the Mississippi River. Then they set out afoot again, walking all the way to Sallisaw, I.T. (now Oklahoma). There they began picking cotton for a full-blooded Indian.

The next spring Grandpa again became restless. He threw their belongings into a tent and burned them up. Afoot, they started back for Tennessee. It must have been an odd sight to see this big, whiskered man walking down the dusty roads with five children strung out behind him, two or three barefooted, all dirty and unkempt.

Grandpa and Daddy carried on their shoulders five-year-old Lucy when she got too tired walking. (Daddy's oldest sister Addie wasn't with them as she had married at a young age before they left Tennessee.)

According to Uncle Brown, when they crossed over to Fayetteville, Arkansas, no one agreed to let them spend the night. Angered, Grandpa told the authorities that unless they found a place for them to stay, he would burn down the town before morning. So they hastened to find an acceptable place for them to bunk and gave them all a warm breakfast the next morning. Some kindhearted people even bought shoes for the barefooted children.

Days later, the motley troop reached Batesville, where Grandpa and the children where hauled into court. An attempt was made to determine his sanity.

"Do you remember the last time you saw your wife?" the judge inquired.

"Oh, yeah, "Grandpa affirmed. "She was on the Good Ship Zion with the Apostle Paul sailing to the Isle of Patmos."

Daddy said he drew up and shivered, for he knew that with an answer like that the kids would be taken from Grandpa's custody. And so they were.

Grandpa was sentenced to one month in jail. Daddy, Aunt Mollie, and Aunt Sarah were each farmed out to separate families. Uncle Brown and Aunt Lucy (the youngest) huddled together holding hands. A kindly man, John Patterson, took them both, realizing how difficult it would be for them if they were separated. (Later the Pattersons purchased and moved to a farm near Dodsonville, Texas.)

Daddy was unhappy with the family to whom he was assigned as he felt they mistreated him. After several months he ran away and rejoined Grandpa. Much later he returned to Tennessee, where he eventually married my mother, Lubie Exie White of Hardin County.

In his latter years, Grandpa's periods of mental imbalance were much less frequent. He sometimes lived for weeks with Mamma and Daddy. On one of those visits he took the cotton hoe from the hands of my pregnant mother and sent her to the house saying, "The field is no place for a woman."

Then in 1925 Grandpa headed for Oklahoma again, probably to visit his brother David Henry. While sleeping by an open campfire, his clothing caught fire, and he was seriously burned. After spending a few days in a hospital at Henryetta, Oklahoma, he died. He is buried somewhere near Holdenville.

Grandpa "Toob" Kennedy

Uncle Cleve Millner and Aunt Mirtie.

Our family under Red River Bridge.

Chapter 4
The Great Depression Hits

From the train coach, we moved into the Milligan house in Dodsonville, close to Aunt Mirtie's family. We enjoyed playing simple games with our cousins, such as hop scotch, skip the rope, and hide-and-seek.

One of my favorite games was Rover-Rover Ante-Over. A ball was thrown over the tin roof of the house. If someone caught it, that person would quickly run around the house and throw the ball at one on the opposite side. If hit, that child was out of the game. The team that won got the others out first.

We began attending a little church in Dodsonville. Though only four years old, I was impressed by the zeal and sincerity of the worshippers. During the song service I would take a book and sing, pretending that I was reading the words. I listened to the preacher, though I probably did not understand very much. Still, I knew this was a solemn and important occasion.

Because of the numerous such experiences I had as a child, I have always had doubts about the wisdom of pulling the children out of the regular worship services with the grownups. I believe I experienced more awe, devotion, and reverence than I ever would have in a Children's Church. Of course, I heard things I did not understand at the time, but none of us fully understand God when we are worshipping.

Another game we children enjoyed playing during the week was church. We would sing songs and even pray. My cousin Madie Caddell was reminiscing during one of my last visits with her.

"L. D.," she said, "even as young as you were, you liked to preach. We would have you stand on a little box and you tried hard to imitate our pastor. We all enjoyed listening to you!"

I remember the first time our preacher came to our house for Sunday dinner. Poor as we were, we felt specially honored to have him. Mamma was an excellent cook. She could make a delicious meal out of the simplest ingredients. I shall never forget that on that day we even had a can of store-bought kraut!

Our parents cautioned us that we must be on our best behavior while the pastor was there. I was afraid to say anything, lest I say the wrong thing. As a boy, the fair skin of my face was so freckled you could hardly touch it with a toothpick without contacting a freckle. I was so self-conscious that I supposed I was the ugliest child on earth. (As I grew older my timidity earned for me the nickname "Shy Pie.") On this day the discerning preacher noticed that I was quiet and withdrawn.

"I never knew a freckled-faced boy who wasn't honest," he said with a smile, as he patted me on the head. He could never know how much those unforgettable words of encouragement meant to me.

"I may never be good-looking, but I will be honest," I determined.

At that time we had no car, so we walked to church. One night during a service there came a Texas cloudburst, probably 15 to 20 inches of water failing during the hour. As we left church, I was terrified at the sight of muddy water running everywhere, deeply covering the little road home. I began to cry for I was afraid I would drown. My big, strong dad reached down, lifted me up, and set me on his secure shoulders.

"Don't worry, L. D.," he promised. "I'll carry you home."

Often when faced with frightening problems, I have remembered that incident and thought, "My heavenly Father is lifting me with his strong arms and reassuring me: 'Don't worry, L. D. I'll carry you.'"

Aunt Mirtie's husband, Uncle Cleve, was a quiet, eccentric little squint-eyed man whose nickname was Nubbin. I never saw him in anything except overalls. A good singer, he liked nothing better than to get out on the porch or under the shade tree in his chair, singing songs from his paperback songbook. He knew his shaped notes and needed no instrumental music.

The Missionary Baptist Church that we all attended had a split. The strife and controversy so depressed Uncle Cleve that he quit going. His family and relatives pled with him to no avail. For years he stayed home while they went on to church. They prayed for him, fearful that he had never been saved.

Years later when Uncle Cleve died, the family were amazed to see a long line of blacks from the community coming to pay their respects. These simple people wept and told Aunt Mirtie how much they loved him. Then they revealed that for years, unbeknown to his family, Uncle Cleve, in his overalls had been slipping off from home to come worship with them at their little black church.

"When he first came, we tried to lay a sheet across the seat for him, but he wouldn't let us," they told his astonished family.

How easy it is to misjudge people who do not conform to our expectations. I still get a lump in my throat when I think of my Uncle Cleve. He was a kind, simple little man who never sought to impress others nor to elevate himself above anyone. He felt at home among the humblest of God's people and in the smallest of churches. (Of course, from God's perspective there are no little people nor little churches.)

Uncle Cleve may wear a white robe in the heavenly choir, but likely he would be as happy in overalls. Just so long as he could be singing for Jesus!

The world began experiencing the Great Depression in 1929. Survival in those difficult days required hard work, creativity, and the most skillful use of one's meager resources. To waste food was considered a sin. Consequently, we were required to eat whatever we put on our plates. (Most of the time we were so hungry that doing so did not pose a problem.)

In the spring we gathered wild greens, such as lambs quarter (of the goosefoot family) and dock (of the buckwheat family). There were two varieties of dock—the broadleaf and the narrowleaf, which we preferred. Boiled slowly with a dollop of pork fatback, these wild greens were quite edible.

A neighbor woman had some tame blackberries. We volunteered to help her pick them, hoping she might give us a couple of handfuls with which to make a blackberry pie. As I helped Mamma pick, I was allowed to eat an occasional berry. I felt certain that anyone who had a blackberry patch must be rich.

We bought our flour in large sacks. When emptied, the white sacks were sewn into pillowcases, sheets, and even underwear. A bit of verse I found reminds me of those simple clothes.

Flour Sack Underwear

Long ago when but a child,
There was no cash to spare,
When my mother carefully sewed
My little flour sack underwear.

The bags that came around our flour,
Were always washed with care,
And very soon I would have
Some brand new underwear.

The lettering did not really fade,
But I really did not care.
It seemed to lend a bit of color
To my flour sack underwear.

Aunt Jemima and Mother's Best
Warmed my sturdy little chest.
Snow White provided the slip I wore
Beneath my Sunday dress.

24

My nightie came to my feet
And wrapped around my shins,
And it was very soft and snuggly,
With Robin Hood beneath my chin.

There was no lace or fancy stitches
On my little flour sack britches,
But Dixie Lilly, pale and neat,
Marched across my little seat.

Many years have come and gone;
Still in my dreams I see
The little flour sack underwear
My mother made for me.

— Author Unknown

To supplement his income, Arthur Gallaway went from house to house selling home products. One day he let us sample a little chocolate milk made from cocoa mix. I thought it tasted heavenly! We children begged Mamma to buy it. While it cost only 10¢ for a fairly large package, Mamma said she couldn't afford it.

I cried in disappointment. But on another day Arthur's boys picked me up and took me to town in their little sports roadster. At the drugstore they treated me to a big cold glass of root beer. This refreshing beverage I had never before tasted.

Not every childhood memory is a pleasant one. When the old folks got together at night they sometimes amused one another by relating gruesome tales they had heard. One of these that scared me was about a man musing as he shaved, "Twenty years ago today I was bit by a mad dog." Then according to the story, by the time he finished shaving he took a rabies fit. I shuddered as I visualized the horror of going mad.

While we had no dogs, I liked them. One day a hound passed through our yard. Glad to see him, I held out my piece of bread to him. As he snatched it, he nipped my finger slightly.

"You'll go mad in seven days," one of my sisters told me. Terrified, I counted the days for the next week and hardly slept at night. I wet my bed and had nightmares. To me, I was surely under a death sentence. At times I stood by my parents' bed crying, begging to get in bed with them. But I would not tell them the cause of my fears, for they had warned me against feeding or playing with strange dogs.

To my great relief, the week passed and I did not take rabies. But after this traumatic experience, I never did like dogs. I also have a slight idea of what it's like to be on death row.

Chapter 5
We Get a Model-T Ford!

The next year we moved to the farm of John and Fannie Patterson, a few miles from Dodsonville. The Pattersons had gone there from Arkansas after getting custody of my Uncle Brown and Aunt Lucy. They sent Uncle Brown to a business college and gave him a good education. He became a telegrapher for the Frisco Railway at age 19. However, Aunt Lucy felt that Fannie did not really want her, so she left and eventually married Arthur Jones.

With a mule-drawn breaking plow, Daddy broke the fields for Mr. Patterson and planted the crops. The rest of us helped in the garden and in chopping and snapping the cotton.

Dad rewarded me for working hard by taking me to the gin with him. It was a pleasure to sit atop the soft cotton that filled the wagon. Then before we returned home, Dad often bought me a grape soda-pop. Sometimes he brought home with him a large basket of inexpensive grapes. The fresh fruit was an unaccustomed delight to us, something we could not afford except at cotton picking time.

Weather in West Texas has always been subject to extremes. Mamma was good at reading signs of change in the skies. On a warm fall morning as we prepared to go to the field, she might caution, "Take your coats and caps for a 'norther' is coming sometime today." Then later we would observe a dark cloudbank in the north moving rather rapidly. When it reached us, we were grateful for our coats. The temperature could drop from the 70 degrees to the 30 degrees in an hour's time. We shivered and ran home.

Before moving from Dodsonville, Dad shocked us all one day. He drove up into the yard in a used 1923 Model-T Ford he had bought for about $125. Now we could go places and do things when we could afford the gas (about 10¢ per gallon).

We frequently visited with our relatives in Dodsonville and with Aunt Lucy and Uncle Arthur Jones, who lived on a farm several miles from us. They had one or two cows, and I loved Aunt Lucy's fresh buttermilk. Mother had taught us children not to ask for any food when we went visiting. But at Aunt Lucy's I sometimes could not resist.

"Ain't Oocy, do you have any buddymilk?" I would quietly inquire if Mamma wasn't around. And she almost always did.

My cousin Marvin Jones, a few years older than I, taught me how to make and shoot a slingshot. I wore my little aviator cap, and thought I was a great hunter. Mamma was pleased at this until she learned we hunted and sometimes killed birds.

One of our favorite excursions in the summer was to Red River. We children played in the dry sandy riverbed but kept a watchful eye out for quick flash floods from above. (I have pictures made in the riverbed with our family and relatives.) Sometimes we were able to find a swimming hole, but we had to check for quicksand first.

Wild plum bushes grew along the sandy banks of Red River. After we picked the plums and took them home, Mamma canned them in her little faithful pressure cooker. In the wintertime it thrilled us when she opened one of the quart or half-gallon jars of delicious fruit. I think the jars were always empty at the end of the meal. Delbert and I would have a little contest to see who had the most plum seeds by his plate.

The summer's heat under our little tin roof was most uncomfortable. So usually we moved a couple of our beds into the yard to feel the night breeze. My brother and I would go to bed first. Many times I put myself to sleep counting not sheep but stars.

One night Delbert and I were awakened by a loud pistol shot. A pack of coyotes had headed toward our house, and there was always the possibility a mad one might be among them. Dad had pulled a pistol from under his pillow and fired it at the pack to turn them. We pulled the blanket over our heads just in case a stray might come by our bed.

In cold weather I watched with trepidation as Daddy tried to crank our Model-T. It sometimes kicked the crank back, almost breaking his arm. But once started, the little car took us to exciting places. Two or three times a year we would drive to Hollis, Oklahoma, to get needed items that weren't available locally. While the scenery wasn't much, we children entertained ourselves by counting the telephone poles along the way.

The social heart of our community was Kelly School, which my sisters attended and where I later got my first year and a half of education. Most of the people in the community turned out for the school plays, singing, and declamation programs. I was so proud of my sisters when they gave speeches and recited poems.

One year Genova gave a moving recitation of Henry Van Dyke's "America For Me." Oreathel listened intently as Genova and the older children practiced their pieces. She quickly learned several of them, even though she was only a small nine-year-old. I would listen in awe and pride as she recited them to me.

Occasionally we visited someone who had a Victrola, around which we sat spellbound. Listening to my favorite singer, Jimmy Rodgers, I soon learned to sing by memory "All Around the Water Tank." Other than the church hymns, this was the first song I ever learned.

On the prairies, roadbanks, and along the edges of fields, tumbleweeds grew freely. These were big round weeds, often two to three feet in diameter. On a still day we children enjoyed stacking them into tumbleweed houses. In autumn they would break off near the ground. It was fun to chase them as they were blown by the wind. If the wind was very strong, we could not catch them. If you've never watched the crazy antics of a tumbleweed, you've missed something.

We had no zoos, nor botanical gardens where we lived, but nature never slighted us. Colorful wildflowers bloomed profusely, especially after a rain. We never had to walk far to find a prairie dog colony. These little squirrel-like rodents entertained us as they frolicked about and emitted their barking cry. They seemed to know we were their friends.

When we drove down the road in our car, we sometimes raced with jack rabbits. For a short distance they would stay ahead of us, even when we were going about 40 miles an hour. These longeared critters have powerful hind legs. While we never ran with wolves, we did enjoy running with the rabbits.

I had one pastime that alarmed my parents and amazed the other children. Barefooted, I would sit quietly on the ground by a colony of large red ants. As I observed them, I allowed them to crawl over my hands, feet, and clothing. They did not sting me, perhaps because I did not fear nor harm them. The industry, strength, and cooperation of these little insects always fascinated me. A few years later when I came across Proverbs 6:6-8, I knew what it was talking about.

Another interesting little friend I made was the horned toad. This ugly little reptile with his flattened body, short tail, and hornlike spikes looked dangerous, but he was not. On the street at Dodsonville we boys sometimes lined up and raced our toads. I don't think mine ever won.

When children today are told to go play, they are apt to protest. "Play! What with? We don't have anything to play with." Has television and affluence robbed them of their creativity? There are yards, fields, flowers, insects, creeks, rocks, trees, and animals today just as when we "depression kids" grew up. Dandelions are just waiting to be strung into crowns for the girls. Four-leaf clovers are lingering to be discovered. Ants, lizards, lightning bugs, and lady bugs are still around to delight a child's heart. Colorful birds and interesting insects flit about, ready to be admired and identified. It's always fun to make toad houses in the wet sand. Grapevine swings are still in the woods.

Today's children have so many toys that mothers trip on them walking through the house. Many of them have their own televisions and VCRs. Yet they stay bored so much of the time. Could it be that they are more deprived than we who grew up poor in material things but rich in creativity and imagination?

I certainly don't mean that the '20s and the '30s were the "good ole days." They were hard, lean, discouraging days. But since the springs of happiness are not outside us, but in our hearts, we found fun, challenge, and excitement in spite of the good things we lacked.

We might escape boredom and unhappiness if we had the positive attitude of the Apostle Paul who said, "I have learned to be content whatever the circumstances."[7]

L.D. and Delbert, about 1928-29.

Delbert and me.

Fate and Lubie Kennedy, my parents.

Treasure In Earthen Vessels

Chapter 6
The Day I'll Never Forget

In 1932 we moved to the Rob Holland Ranch. Daddy fed the horses and cleaned the stables. In season we farmed.

A month before my seventh birthday, I started to school at Kelly, a little two-room building. I was so hungry to learn that I usually stayed in at recess rather than going out to play. The large, colorful reading charts that I had watched the older children use always fascinated me. Soon I had gone through my primer and first grade readers and was using a second grade reader. (At that time in Texas, schools permitted pupils to complete more than one grade per year if they were able. Likewise, upon finishing the 11th grade, one was a high school graduate.)

I was so fortunate to have as my teacher R. H. (Bob) Birchfield, a brilliant young man who was kind, understanding, knowledgeable, and interesting. He was about 18 or 19, and Kelly was his first teaching assignment after completing his B.A. degree from the University of Texas.

When Mr. Birchfield was a child, an angry sow had bitten off most of his fingers. But he managed to write beautifully with the stubs that remained. One day he wrote the ABCs on the blackboard and instructed us first graders to copy them on our tablets. I was good at reading, but writing was not my thing! Laboriously I pushed my penny cedar pencil upon the rough tablet sheet in front of me. But the letters I made hardly resembled the beautiful ones on the board. I was embarrassed and frightened as my teacher walked down my aisle inspecting our work. In desperation I tried harder. That only made things worse.

Tearfully, I blurted out, "I can't do it. Daddy wouldn't get me a good pencil and tablet like I wanted."

"There now," he tried to comfort me, as he patted me on the head. "There's nothing wrong with your pencil or paper. Just hold the pencil naturally with your fingers and let me show you something."

Gently, Mr. Birchfield placed his hands on top of mine. I looked down and to my amazement beautiful letters were appearing on my rough tablet sheet.

"I can write!" I thought. Yet it was not I, but my teacher writing through my hand.

Years later it occurred to me that this memorable incident was a striking analogy of salvation and the Christian life. Paul wrote in Galatians, "I am crucified with Christ: nevertheless I live; yet not I, but Christ liveth in me: and the life which I now live in the flesh I live by the faith of the Son of God, who loved me, and gave himself for me.[8]

We can no more live the Christian Life ourselves than we could save ourselves in the first place. It all comes about as we trust Christ, quit trying to do it ourselves, and yield to him. The fruit of the Spirit is not a product of our zeal and efforts but of Christ who lives in us.

Fifty years after I was in the first grade I went back to the Kelly Community, talking with several families there. The old schoolhouse was long gone. But I was thrilled when Miss Rama Camp informed me that Mr. Birchfield was still living and gave me his address in Amarillo. We began corresponding and a few years later I visited this remarkable man. I thanked him for helping instill in me a love for learning and getting me off to such a good start in school.

It was no surprise to learn that Mr. Birchfield had become a well-known educator in Texas and for 29 years had been principal of the San Jacinto School in Amarillo.

While I attended Kelly School we sometimes heard whoops and shouts, looked out our windows, and watched real cowboys bringing by herds of long-horned cattle. This was more exciting than later watching cattle drives on the movie screens.

Children then brought their lunches to school in a paper bag or lunch bucket. Occasionally we swapped lunches, broadening our eating experiences. From one of the swaps I tasted my first grapefruit. I got biscuits with "coon" meat from another. When I went home, I excitedly told my parents of my enjoyable trade. I liked it better than jack rabbit meat.

Dust storms were quite common in West Texas in the '30s. (Kansas and Oklahoma had suffered droughts, and the dry topsoil was blown our way.) When our teachers knew one was coming, they dismissed school.

If we didn't make it home before the worst part of the storm hit, we got into a ditch, closed our eyes, and put our noses close to the ground. The first time I had to do this I was most frightened.

The Rob Holland family lived in a nice brick house, but after one of these storms they said they could write their names on the furniture. One day while I was home a dust storm hit. Looking out a window I could scarcely make out the nearby haystack in our yard.

I was the "fraidycat" of our family. My parents would reassure me and try to explain away my fears. Sometimes Dad would offer me a dime (more than a dollar now!) to go by myself on a dark night and hang a piece of paper on the windmill. Though tempted, I was often too fearful to take him up on his offer. I was afraid I might meet a mad dog.

Our parents taught us to respect all adults, especially the elderly. It was a pleasure to take food to them that Mamma had cooked. Often I accompanied Mamma on her visits. One of my favorite old widows usually served me milk and tea cakes. Then she let me play with her wooden spools and colorful buttons. I could have entertained myself with them for hours.

There had been tuberculosis in Mamma's family, and she herself had weak lungs. Having heard raw eggs would help prevent tuberculosis, I became the champion raw egg sucker of our community. Women usually gave me an egg or two for crawling under their house or barn and gathering eggs that had been laid there. They were amused at seeing me stick a pin hole in the end of the egg and suck out its content. One day I sucked 12 eggs with no ill

effects. So far, I've had no lung problems—nor high cho-
lesterol.

I was fortunate to grow up in a godly home where our
parents modeled the Christian life for us children. Bible
reading, family prayer, and spiritual conversation were as
much a part of our daily lives as food, water, or sleep.
Regardless of how tired or sleepy we were, we joined in
family worship before retiring. Our parents encouraged us
to ask questions or make comments.

One morning Delbert and I were playing in the yard
when we heard muffled sounds coming from our storm
cellar. Softly we crept up to it to investigate. Then we heard
our weeping mother praying earnestly to God. When she
called my name and asked God to save me, I trembled with
gratitude and excitement. It makes a lasting impression on
a child to slip up on his mother and hear her beseeching
God on his behalf.

We frequently attended cottage prayer meetings.
Sometimes I grew tired, but usually I was moved by the
prayers and testimonies. One day my parents broke the
news to me that my Sunday School teacher, a lovely lady
of about 16 years, had died during a tonsillectomy. Even
though I felt sadness and fear, they took me to her funeral. On the way home I was somber as I considered how
death comes to the young as well as the old. Perhaps I
would die while still young!

Then I began reflecting upon my own life. Knowing the
hopes and expectations of my parents, I tried to impress
others with the fact that I was a "good boy." But I knew
better. By the time I was six years old, I knew that when
the Bible said, "For all have sinned, and come short of the
glory of God..."[9] it meant L. D. Kennedy too. I knew that I
had evil thoughts, desires, and imaginations. Sometimes I
lied to my parents or disobeyed them. I lived in constant
dread of death, the second coming of Christ, and the judg-
ment.

Gradually, in family worship and church services my
hypocrisies were exposed. My conscience was often smit-

ten with guilt. Fears increased as I learned the Biblical truth that "the wages of sin is death..."[10]

Sometimes at night I could not sleep, for it seemed like the devil was sitting on one of my bed posts leering at me. "If you die tonight, you'll go to hell," he seemed to say. I knew it was so. I felt the terrible separation that sin brings. Separation from God, from my family, and from peace.

Unbeknown to me, I was experiencing what the Christians of our community called "conviction for sin."

About that time the little Methodist Church in town had a "revival meeting." We attended some of the services. On Sunday morning I riveted my attention on the words of the old-time evangelist. It has been a long time ago, so I can't remember the particulars of his sermon. But I believe he took us to Calvary and had us focus our attention upon the Man on the middle cross.

I was amazed and grateful when it dawned upon me that Christ died for my sins. But I still felt no peace for I knew I was unfit for heaven. Then somehow the truth came through that justification is by faith in Him and not by our good deeds nor worthiness. For the first time I realized that salvation was not a reward for being good, but the free gift of God. Joyfully, I saw that He had swapped placed with us. As Paul wrote, "God made him who had no sin to be sin for us, so that in him we might become the righteousness of God."[11]

I trusted Christ as Savior, received Him by faith, and passed from death into life. Pressing my father's hand, I told him I wanted "to go forward."

"Are you sure you know what you are doing?" he asked.

"Yes! I've been saved."

I made my profession of faith but did not join the church for my parents had taught us that baptism was by immersion. I wanted to be sure.

When I took that simple step of faith, joy, peace, and love flooded my being. No longer was I afraid of dying nor going to hell. That same week I began sharing with my family and schoolmates how wonderful it was to be a Christian.

Now I know I was young then — only seven years old. Had I been given a doctrinal examination at that time, I could not have passed it. I had read very little of the Bible. Many things I did not understand. But I did know that I was going to heaven. I also knew that from that day forward the life of L. D. Kennedy would be under new management. Jesus was Lord.

Over the years people have sometimes asked me, "How can you say for sure you are going to heaven? That sounds like boasting."

I have replied, "The sins Jesus took upon himself were not his but mine. The righteousness I have is not the righteousness of L. D. Kennedy but his righteousness imputed to me by faith. So I'm not boasting about myself but about my Savior."

Upon going home from church, I did a thing very uncharacteristic of me. It was my assigned job to feed our chickens and provide them with fresh, clean water. Their watering troughs were Model-T "caissons" (tires) split in half. Whenever the chickens came for a drink, they liked to walk about in the tire troughs with their dirty smelly feet. I detested cleaning the "caissons" out and shirked it whenever possible.

But this day I knelt by the tires and scrubbed them with my hands. Then I went to the windmill and brought back the cool, fresh water, just pumped. After pouring it into their troughs, I found myself apologizing to the chickens for the way I had neglected them in the past. I told them I was a "saved" boy and would take better care of them thereafter. I know this may sound absurd, but it's exactly what happened.

That was a day I shall never forget!

Chapter 7

To Bogota and the Booger Farm

After a year on the Holland Ranch, Dad grew restless and decided to return to Tennessee. Mamma cried. She would have to leave Aunt Mirtie and her family. We children were sad too. Aunt Mirtie's girls were almost like sisters to us, and we didn't know if we would ever see them again. We hated to leave Kelly School and the friends we had made there and around Dodsonville.

During the summer Mamma had worked hard canning about 200 jars of vegetables and fruit. The depression was severe in 1932, so she had to sell them for a few cents per jar.

We sold or gave away most of our household goods. Then the six of us piled into our old Model-T and drove to Bogota, Tennessee. It took three long days.

Bogota was a small, unincorporated village, ten miles north of Dyersburg on Highway 78. Before reaching it, you must go down a bluff and cross the Obion River. When we lived in Bogota, it had two grocery stores (one of which also housed a post office), a taxi stand, a cotton gin, and two small churches (Methodist and Church of Christ).

Bogota (with accent on the second syllable) got its name from an amiable South American who worked at the nearby sawmill. From Bogota, Columbia, he couldn't speak English. His fellowworkers liked this little foreigner. So the village bears the mispronounced name of Bogota, Columbia.

We unloaded at the home of Aunt Addie Scott, Daddy's widowed sister. It was January, 1933. Trees and woods were all around. Accustomed to the wide open plains of Texas, I at first experienced some claustrophobia. To

breathe more freely and see a greater distance, I sometimes climbed to the top of tall trees.

Grandma Bashebe was now living with Aunt Addie, so
we had the privilege of getting to know her. She had finally divorced Grandpa Kennedy on grounds of desertion and
married an old girlhood sweetheart, Jeff Caudel, who had
lost his wife several years before. Grandpa Caudel was
now dead.

Aunt Addie's daughter Mirtle died giving birth to her
first child, Willie White. Aunt Addie kept him and raised
him as one of her own sons. So J. V. (just a bit older than
he), Finis, and Floyd were like brothers to him.

When I started to school at Bogota, they found I could
read on a fourth or fifth grade level, so they put me in the
fourth grade. It was the middle of the school year, and I
was overwhelmed by arithmetic, which I had never before
had. I cried and begged until Principal McKnight put me
back into grade three.

Another reason I wanted in the third grade was so I
would be in the room with Willie. There was a custom then
at Bogota of the other boys whipping a new boy who
enrolled. I was small and didn't know how to fight. But
Willie and J. V. were strong and would come to my rescue
when I called for them. J. V. was a quiet, peaceful young-
ster, but powerful and devastating when stirred up. He
was so strong he was nicknamed Tarzan. Soon the other
boys learned to leave me alone.

In our room was a big, tall boy (said to be 21) who came
to school barefooted even in the snow. The soles of his feet
were so thick he could put them against a hot stove for
awhile without burning them. He had a crush on our
young teacher, Miss Grace Tillman, perhaps because she
was so kind to him.

Not wishing to impose upon Aunt Addie, we moved to
the Booger Farm, northwest of Bogota. (I suppose it got its
name from being so swampy and isolated. Or maybe it was
because nobody but "us boogers" lived there.) The dirt
road coming to our house was often impassable. Then we

walked on logs or planks across the dredge ditches to get to school.

It was winter and we had no work. Daddy took his little single-shot Winchester rifle or pearl-handled 45-pistol and hunted rabbits, squirrels, "coon," and "possums" for our meat. One day he brought Mamma an old long-neck swamp bird.

"Are you sure it's o.k. to eat?" she asked him.

"Oh, sure," he replied. "Any bird is eatable."

Mamma cooked the bird for supper, but it was a so tough we couldn't chew it. At least we enjoyed the broth with our biscuits.

"I'm going to boil it tomorrow. Then it will be tender," Mamma assured us. But even after she had done that, it was so tough we couldn't chew it. In disgust she grabbed the fowl by the legs and threw it out the back door.

"Don't ever bring another one of those birds in here for me to cook!" she ordered Daddy.

Willie became as close as a brother to Delbert and me. In rainy weather we boys played under our house. (It was about four or five feet off the ground to protect from flooding.) We built farms and roads in the dirt. We made the chugging sounds of cars as we traveled over these roads with our snuff, medicine, and flavoring bottles. We harvested our cotton and took it to the gin. When tired of this we invented other games.

Sometimes at night our parents played dominoes or checkers with us. Daddy often entertained us with stories. We sang together. We read books. It was fun to be part of such a close-knit family.

Daddy was a brilliant and knowledgeable thinker. He was such an avid reader that he inspired us children to love books. Having finished only the fifth grade, he had never studied algebra. But when my sisters brought him algebra problems that had them baffled, he usually would get the correct answer by arithmetic.

Mamma had just a fourth grade education, but she wanted us children to finish grade school at least. To encourage us boys to do our homework, she and Daddy bought a wicker library table of about five-feet length. Delbert and I did our homework on it, propping our feet on the round that went from end-to-end. A kerosene lamp in its center gave us plenty of light.

When visiting Willie, we boys enjoyed sitting on Aunt Addie's front porch and teasing Grandma Bashebe. We had heard you couldn't get her to speak a bad word about anyone. So we mentioned to her the meanest men in our community.

"He's an evil man, isn't he Grandma?"

"Oh I don't know about that," she would answer. Then she would say something good about him, such as "He is a hard worker" or "He sure whistles pretty." Grandma died in August 1933 at age 67. She was the only grandparent I ever knew, and it was for so brief a time. We marveled at her kindness, mercy, and patience. Had I known her longer, I could have learned much from her.

The next year we moved into a little bungalow south of Bogota. We were proud to have people visit us there, for it was a comfortable, well-built house, not just a "shotgun shack." Daddy made a sharecrop for Bunyan McBride, a police officer in Memphis.

We boys insisted it was our inalienable right to go barefooted on the first day of spring, regardless of the temperature. "You'll catch a death of cold," Mamma sometimes warned us. But I don't recall doing so.

Exploring our area, we found grapevine swings, persimmons, muscadine grapes (from which Mamma made tantalizing jelly and preserves), wild small-seeded blackberries, hickory nut and black walnut trees. These were delights that we never had in West Texas. We played a game we called "Tarzaning trees." It was fun to climb to the top of saplings, especially birch, and bend them to the ground. Dad taught us to hunt, fish, and trap.

Because there was a rough, homemade boat at Possum Pond, Delbert and I often fished there. One day I laid my straw hat on a hollow cypress stump in the water before we set out our floats for catching catfish. There was a hole in the bottom of the boat, but I stopped the leak by applying my bare heel to it. When we were ready to leave the pond, we rowed by the stump to get my hat. As I lifted it up, I was horrified to see a poisonous water moccasin coiled under the shade of my big hat.

Quickly I lunged to the other end of our boat, deserting the big hole I had plugged with my heel. Water rushed in and soon the little boat began sinking. Delbert and I "abandoned ship" and swam desperately to the bank. Perhaps the snake was so frightened as we for we saw no more of him.

Sometimes Daddy and a few of our relatives would grabble for fish in holes along the bank. I've heard them shout, "Watch out! Here comes a snake," as they threw it over their shoulder. And sure enough, it was. They claimed that snakes wouldn't bite under water, but I never believed that.

One of our fields ran along Highway 78. "Keep your eyes on the cotton row, and don't watch cars," Daddy would instruct us. He promised to take us swimming in the Obion River on the 4th of July if our cotton crop was chopped and laid by. So we tried to keep our eyes off the cars.

When an infrequent airplane flew over, however, we stopped, looked a moment, and waved. I never dreamed that years later I would be riding planes over most of the United States and a number of foreign countries.

One day Daddy was sharpening a hoe in the cotton field. His hand slipped and he cut his wrist. Blood squirted everywhere. Calmly he stopped it with his thumb and went to the house where he asked Mamma for a needle and thread. With her assistance he sutured the cut and stopped the bleeding. Then he applied kerosene generously, wrapped it in a piece of white sheet, and went back to the field. During the hardships of his childhood he had learned to meet pain and emergencies unperturbed.

Even after working in the field all day, we children had assigned home chores. In the field we might have complained about being tired. But at quitting time our energy returned quickly. As soon as we completed our chores, Delbert and I would rush to the yard. We would play pitch or bat fly balls to one another until dark overtook us.

One evening when Delbert was about seven, we were playing ball with a group of boys at Bogota. Delbert was hit in the mouth by a baseball bat, breaking his gums and knocking loose all his front teeth. He bled so profusely I feared he would faint, but he was a tough kid. Dad was at work when we reached home. Mother sent for him. He took Delbert to a doctor in Dyersburg. We all prayed earnestly. Miraculously my little brother lost none of his teeth.

Though pressured to make a livelihood, Dad found time to do things with us children besides work. That meant more than anything he could have bought us. As a young man he had enjoyed playing baseball. He could still throw curves and drop balls and was a good hitter. He taught Delbert and me how to do the same.

He did have at least one weakness: he chewed tobacco and smoked a pipe sometimes. One day he sent me to J. W. Hopper's General Store in Bogota to get him a plug of Brown Mule chewing tobacco. My reward was a penny with which to buy a long "all-day" sucker. (More than once I had washed or dried dishes for my older sister Genova in order to get a penny sucker.)

During the long walk home, I enjoyed my sucker. But as I held the tobacco, curiosity got the best of me: I wanted to know how it tasted. So I broke off a little corner of it and chewed it. I became so sick and dizzy that I never wanted to do that again.

Desperate times sometimes produce desperate men. Mother's brother Uncle Worley White went to Hopper's Store and asked to charge a 48-pound sack of flour.

"I'm sorry, but I can't charge it," Mr. Hopper contended. "You have too much in credit already."

"But we are out of food at my house and my family are hungry."

"I'm sorry, but I can't charge it."

Uncle Worley threw the sack of flour over his shoulder and exclaimed, "Then I'm taking it and don't you try to stop me! I'll pay you when I get the money." Mr. Hopper was too decent to shoot a man for a sack of flour, so he let him go.

We were poor but Daddy was proud. He would not work on the W.P.A. (which he scornfully referred to as "We Piddle Around.") Neither would he take free food from the Red Cross. In the hot summer, after crops were laid by, he and I would take a pole axe and crosscut saw to the nearby thickets and cut stove wood. We sold it for 75¢ a rick.

He trapped all kinds of wild animals and sold the furs to Sears Roebuck. (They brought a good price for those days.) I helped him put the furs on boards to stretch. Then we hung them on the side of an outbuilding to dry and cure out. I enjoyed running the wooden box rabbit traps Dad had made for me.

Once we had no food. Daddy prayed earnestly that God would help him get a fish to feed his hungry family. Then he took a boat to a nearby corn field covered with backwater from the Obion River. Soon he gigged a huge, bony carp. He and mother cleaned and mealed it, and she cooked it. Before eating it, we all bowed our heads while Daddy led a sincere prayer of thanks.

On several occasions Dad saved my life. Once when the backwater was out our family were wading down the road. (This was before I had learned to swim.) The water was only waist deep, but suddenly I stepped off into a deep branch from which the bridge had washed away. Confident that Dad would help me, I held my breath. He pulled me out by the hair of my head.

In the summertime men from the community would erect a large brush arbor. There would be revival service every night for a month or longer. Usually the preachers were Pentecostals. There was no Baptist church in Bogota, so we attended most of the services. Shouting and tongue-speaking were common under the arbor.

Daddy and Mamma cautioned us about the extreme emotionalism and claims of sinless perfection. One of our neighbors shouted at the revival and claimed he had been sanctified. The next week in his field we heard him cursing his horses. My parents had no confidence in that kind of religion.

The Holiness preachers visited in our home and sometimes spent the night with us. Daddy knew the Bible better than they and enjoyed engaging them in discussion. We children sat quietly and listened. Usually our understanding of salvation, security, and true Biblical holiness were strengthened.

Prophecy preaching was popular then as it is now. Franklin D. Roosevelt was called "the antichrist" and his program of NRA (National Recovery Administration) was deciphered as 666, the number of the beast in Revelation 13. NRA was printed on many packages, goods, and products. We were told we would take the "mark of the beast" if we used any of those items.

At that time there was a patent medicine for sore throat named 666. I cried in protest when Mamma started to give it to Delbert and me one night. She reassured us that no Christian would take the "mark of the beast."

The sad truth is that the ones who preach most on prophecy often know the least about it. They appeal to the pride, carnality, and curiosity of their hearers by claiming to reveal deep mysteries and secrets of prophecy. Yet most of what they teach is borrowed from some book other than the Bible or from mere guesswork.

Over the years I have heard prophecy preachers identify as the antichrist Hitler, Mussolini, Hirohito, Stalin, Khomenei, Kissinger, or the pope. They took Old Testament prophecies that were fulfilled before or around the first coming of Christ and squeezed out of the passages Germany, Russia, China, Iran, the USA, the League of Nations, or the European Commonmarket.

I have seen the elaborate eschatological charts of these prophets and heard their dogmatic predictions. Usually it has proved to be only vain speculations. Jesus taught that no man knows the day of his return "no, not the angels which are in heaven, neither the Son, but the Father."[12]

Of course, Jesus is coming again and it may be soon. Instead of speculating and date-setting we need to do what he admonished. Watch with alertness. Worship regularly. Work with zeal. And wait with patience and assurance.

The more I observed my father, the more my respect for him grew. One winter he and some neighbors were building a barn near our house. It was cold. One of the workers pulled out a bottle of whiskey, took a drink, and passed it around.

"This will warm you up," he promised.

From a distance I watched out of the corner of my eye. When the bottle reached Daddy, he shook his head and declined. His courageous example later fortified me in times of temptation.

At the little country school at Bogota we were blessed with some competent, caring teachers. Miss Faustine Featherstone lovingly guided us through the fourth grade. In the fifth grade our teacher began each class session with a made-up story that always had a moral. Most of the class liked her suspenseful stories better than Bible readings and were seldom tardy. This class helped increase my love for literature.

At school programs Oreathel was asked to recite poems. Her previous training in Texas helped her become a favorite participant in such programs. I wasn't the only one who wept when she tearfully recited Lillian Leveridge's sentimental war poem, "A Cry From the Canadian Hills." Almost everywhere we went after that, people asked her to give it. I was proud of her.

In the little schools then we had to be on our guard against head lice and itch. One day a friend with itch picked up one of my school books. Carefully I took it home and paid Genova 3¢ to wash the covers with water and lye soap.

As Christmas approached, our parents told us they just couldn't afford to buy us presents. We were disappointed, but understood. Yet on Christmas Day each of us was given a simple, inexpensive gift. Mine was a lovely little green glass giraffe. Proudly, I carried it about and treasured it more than some boys these days would a bicycle or BB gun.

Yes, we were poor, but we didn't wallow in self-pity. Most of the people we knew were poor too. I was not ashamed of my family. I was not ashamed of my patched overalls and bare feet. I had a good self-image. From Christian teachings at home and at school I knew that God had created me so I was somebody important.

Chapter 8

Summer Fun and Fall Drudgery

Our next move was to the Campbell Brown Road east of Bogota. Daddy had decided we would fare better working by the day than sharecropping.

Overseer of the large Campbell Brown farm was Cousin Allen Walker. To have us available to work for him, he furnished us a little rent-free house on the upper Campbell Brown Road and the next year on the lower road. I liked living in these places, for we were near the Obion River.

With Willie, J. V., and other friends, Delbert and I (not yet teenagers) spent many happy days swimming and fishing in the Obion River. There were magical nights when we would borrow a neighbor's unlocked boat, put out some trot lines, and fish until we got too sleepy.

Occasionally we plucked a few ears of someone's corn and roasted it in the sand under our campfire. When it was done, we peeled the shuck back and ate the delicious, juicy kernels. Often we caught fish, but it didn't really make all that much difference.

Once a group of us young boys got permission to have an all night outing at the swampy Bayou west of Bogota. We took a big skillet, lard, meal, seasoning, and coffee. We had no doubts that we would catch plenty of fish.

But large red crawfish (crayfish) kept stealing our bait. We were getting hungry and had no food. Finally, one of us remarked that we had heard crawfish tails were good to eat. So slowly we pulled up the big crustaceans, until we had a bucketful. Those savory mealed, fried tails were the closest thing to shrimp any of us had ever eaten.

The boys had a big laugh when I made a misstep and fell in the Bayou. I simply wrung out my clothes, hung them on a bush near the fire, and dried them.

51

We had no television nor radio at that time, but we did have fun. At the barn we would join in corncob fights. If you got hit, you were out of the game.

Unable to afford firecrackers, we learned how to wrap cloth tightly around a rock, soak the balls briefly in kerosene, light them with a match, and throw fireballs across the night sky. We especially enjoyed doing this at Christmas.

A favorite game was Cowboys and Indians. We made guns out of pieces of wood, clothes pins, and strips of rubber cut from old inner tubes. When I shot someone, I would cry triumphantly, "I shot you!"

"You didn't either!" he would shout back.

For spears we threw long, dry hollow weeds. Mother stopped that game when one of the "spears" cut a gash in my cheek. We tried not to hurt one another, but children will have accidents.

We didn't have bicycles then. But we had heated races rolling old discarded tires around the house and down the road. We also raced on stilts, which we called "tom-walkers." We made these from poles fitted with a crude footrest.

It's hard to satisfy children anymore. They watch TV and videos for hours at a time and want everything they see advertised on children's programs. Then after they have had it awhile, they want to discard it and get something newer.

On Sunday afternoons we had a little community worship service at the Bogota schoolhouse. Daddy taught the adult Sunday School class, which I sometimes attended. His breadth and depth of Biblical understanding were amazing. He was known and respected throughout our community.

Cotton picking began in late August. Needing our wages, our family usually kept us out of school until most of the cotton had been harvested. This was around Thanksgiving or early December. We then studied hard to catch up with the rest of our classes, and none of us ever failed a grade.

The big fields of cotton with green leaves and white bolls were a beautiful sight. But gathering the crop was backbreaking work. And the sharp spurs at the end of the cotton bolls scratched and pierced our fingers until they got tough. At the end of the day, we sometimes soaked our bloodied hands in kerosene (the poor man's medicine).

Mother and Daddy arose about 3:30 or 4:00 a.m. Soon afterwards mother laid out for us a strengthening breakfast of hot biscuits, eggs, hand-churned butter, and sorghum molasses. Many mornings we had "thick'ning gravy," made from lard, flour, and milk. (Those who blamed President Hoover for the Depression called it "Hoover gravy." But I liked it, and still do. Except now we use canola oil instead of lard.)

After picking Allen Walker's cotton, we often drove to fields in adjoining counties. Sometimes more than 100 pickers would be in one large field. In his head Daddy kept up with the cotton weights of each member of his family. At the end of the day he knew the total pounds of each and of his family as a whole. The farmers we picked for often marveled at this.

We tried to be in the cotton field at break of day. By sundown it was not so much our cotton sacks as we pickers who dragged. But our spirits were lifted somewhat by hearing the old Negro spirituals hummed and sung by black pickers in our fields as the day came to its close.

Some mornings we had to wait for dew or frost to dry off the cotton before beginning to pick. At other times we pulled cotton when the ground was frozen because it would be too wet to go down the rows after the ground thawed. When we children wanted to build a fire at the end of the row, Dad seldom would allow. He would tell us to warm ourselves by running up and down a middle between rows that had already been picked. We couldn't protest too loudly when we recalled how Daddy slept on frozen ground when he was our age.

If a cotton sack wore too thin or suffered a snag, it had to be repaired that night. Many times I've watched my tired parents sew the coarse ducking under a coal-oil lamp, fingers stiff from their hard day's work.

Laborers received little money for their efforts—generally $1.00 to $2.00 per hundred pounds of cotton. The average worker picked about 200 pounds a day. With extra effort I tried to exceed 300. When each sack was filled with cotton (60-75 pounds), the picker had to lift it up, throw it across his back, and carry it to the wagon for weighing. Then he climbed into the wagon and emptied it.

I have often said that cotton picking would make or break your back. Fortunately, it seemed to strengthen mine.

Bogota had no school buses so we walked about two miles to school. When the weather was snowy or bitter cold, we stopped at a neighbor's house along the way and warmed ourselves. No one seemed to mind. This kept our hands and feet from getting frostbitten. We looked forward to returning home, for we knew Mamma would be there and give us refreshments. Sometimes it was tea cakes and milk; other times, sorghum and a biscuit left from breakfast.

In the winter Dad would go out with his trusted 22-rifle and kill swamp rabbits. (The shells were much cheaper than shotgun shells, and he was a good shooter.) We ground the rabbits into sausage patties and Mamma canned them. They served as a good substitute for the pork which we did not have.

When the farmers had harvested their corn, Daddy sometimes got permission for us to glean corn that had been missed. I remember doing this once on Christmas day. The down-row was usually most productive. Then we would take the corn to the mill, where it was ground into meal for us on the halves.

Sometimes I suffered from a kind of acute indigestion. Using a recipe obtained from an Indian woman in Texas, Mamma made a pokeberry wine and had me drink one or two tablespoons before each meal. Knowing that pokeberries were considered poisonous, I wondered if the brew would kill me. It didn't! Soon my chronic indigestion was gone, and it never returned.

From such experiences, I learned that not all medical knowledge is confined to the private domain of physicians.

Chapter 9
The 1937 Flood

December, 1936, was a wet month. Then throughout January it rained almost every day. Waters from the Ohio River and other northern streams poured into the Mississippi River. Soon our Obion River (about a mile from our house) could no longer empty into the "Father of Waters." As it was pushed back, it began flooding the lowlands. Then the Mississippi River broke over its levies, and the "Great Flood" became a reality.

We hastily moved much of our household goods to our little upstairs. Daddy tied mattresses and quilts to the rafters of our roof. Before the waters cut us off, we rushed to Aunt Addie's house at a high spot in Bogota. Besides us, she kindly scrouged in three families of relatives.

Daddy paddled back to our flooded house in a wooden boat, bringing back our chickens and cow. He sold most of the chickens and built a scaffold in Aunt Addie's garage where the cow was kept.

One night we heard the flood break across Highway 78 and head in our direction. Soon the water was lapping against the floor of Aunt Addie's house. On a bitter cold day we paddled out to the Church of Christ. Built on a knoll, it was the highest spot in Bogota. For awhile we stayed there with many other refugees.

Of course, there were no indoor toilets. At separate corners of the room someone hanged up quilts, writing "Men" on one and "Women" on the other. A few bedchambers (pots) were placed behind each quilt. When you used one, you took it and threw the contents outside into the backwater.

Those were dreadful days for us. The rains continued and the floods rose. Some people were anxiously counting the days, arguing God would not allow them to exceed the

40 days and nights of rain that produced the flood in Noah's day.

The government had sent in a few motorboats to evacuate marooned people. Voices of desperate people wafted across the water.

"Help! Help! Oh, please, somebody help us," cried Pete Thomas. His mother and little brother were on a kitchen table in their flooded upstairs. To make himself heard, he had crawled out a window onto their roof.

Hearing such calls and the screams of frightened women caused my half-uncle Elmer Caudel to have a mental breakdown, from which he never fully recovered.

Finally, we were evacuated from the Church of Christ. Since we were allowed to bring out only the clothes on our bodies, we wore out two dresses, or two shirts and pants, and two pair of socks. A deputy sheriff stood at the front of the boat to screen who got on, starting with the sick, the elderly, then women and children. Daddy had to come later.

As our heavily-loaded little boat hit the swift channel of the Obion, it was pulled downstream. We didn't know whether we would make it. I was most frightened for Mamma, since we children were better swimmers than she.

We already knew what it was like to be a poor migrant. Now we would learn something about being a refugee.

Along with scores of other families, we went to the gymnasium of Dyersburg High School, where we stayed two or three nights. We were issued one mattress per family. Our family included sister Genova and Robert Whitmore, whom she had married. The mattresses were placed about three feet apart. We sat on the edges and took turns sleeping. The hot soup we were served kept up our strength.

Next we were transferred to a former cigar factory. There we were vaccinated for smallpox, typhoid fever, etc. Armed National Guardsmen were posted within the building and the doors kept locked. When Daddy learned that the water had receded from the Trenton highway, he persuaded a man to take us to the home of Uncle Walter White, a brother of Mamma. Daddy went to Trenton once a week, where he was given a little money to buy food for the family.

For the short period of time we stayed at Uncle Walter's, we children went to a little one-room school in that community. I always dreaded changing schools. We had to accustom ourselves to new books, students, and teachers.

One thing I did like was helping Uncle Walter with his cows. The tinkling of their cowbells was one of the sweetest sounds imaginable. You could identify each cow by the different sound of her bell. Sometimes I rode one of the cows back from the far side of the pasture, but I "caught it" from Mamma if she found out.

Milking some cows was not a pleasant task. It is humiliating to be swatted in the face with a wet cow tail full of cockleburs. Occasionally a cow would kick her bucket, splashing the milk in my face. I learned to bury my head in the cow's flank so I could tell if she started to kick. If she kicked anyway, I sometimes kicked back. That seemed to discourage her from further aggression.

The backwater went down. Caved in portions of Highway 78 were repaired. So about February 20, Cousin Finis Scott came after us in his car and took us back to Aunt Addie's.

Four days later our beloved 48-year-old father died unexpectedly. He had gone to try to salvage some things from the upstairs of our old flood-wracked house on Campbell Brown Road. It had been washed off its blocks and the water had gotten nearly two-feet deep upstairs.

As he pulled on the mattresses and bed clothing, something traumatic happened to him. Some say he had a stroke. Others say it was a brain hemorrhage brought on by the roof collapsing on him.

A strong man, he managed to get out of the house and walk the short distance to Allen Walker's. He went to the stock watering trough, washed his face, and walked into the house. Allen's wife Lubie (named after my mother) met him.

"He had a very strange look on his face," Lubie later told us. "I knew something was wrong."

Slowly he handed her his billfold.

"I'm dying," he said softly. "Give this to my Lubie when she comes."

Then he lay across the bed and within a few moments he was dead. He got his oft-stated wish of dying with his boots on.

I was 12-years-old when Daddy died. Judged by the standards of this world, he was a poor man and a failure. The government thinks of an estate as tangibles such as money, land, stocks, bonds, collectibles, jewelry. Dad left us none of these except the clothes on our backs, $49 in money, and a 1923 Model-T Ford which had set for weeks under the backwater.

But, oh, what a rich intangible legacy he left us. From him we learned honesty, industry, humility, responsibility, and reverence. He was a wise and godly man who emphasized spiritual values above those temporal and material. As Solomon once said, "There is one who considers himself rich, yet has nothing; and one who considers himself poor, yet possesses great wealth."[13]

I am more proud to have been the son of a godly, honest, affectionate Christian sharecropper than I would had my father been a wealthy banker or landowner who lived only for fleshly comforts and material possessions.

In a matter of a few weeks I lost three people who were dear to me. Pneumonia took the life of my young cousin J. V. Then Daddy died. Shortly thereafter James Welch, a schoolmate, was killed in an accident on Highway 78 near Cockleburr. I faced squarely the realities of life and death, and an early manhood was thrust upon me.

Chapter 10
Living in a Schoolhouse

After Daddy's death Mamma wanted to move from the bottoms to hill country. This posed a problem, for we could pay very little rent. Soon we settled for Ferguson schoolhouse, a vacant building about one and a half miles north of Dyersburg. Rent was $5.00 per month.

A prosperous neighbor, Mr. Journey, promised to give us plenty of work. Mrs. Lucy Hart, head of the Dyer County Red Cross, replaced some of the bare essentials for our housekeeping. The building had a vestibule and two large rooms. We used only one of the rooms.

Delbert and I were fascinated by the spacious school yard with a basketball goal and room for a baseball diamond. In rain or wintry weather we played in the adjoining vacant room. Soon our home and yard became a popular playing-place for boys about our age.

It was different with 16-year-old Oreathel. She cried with humiliation, thinking boys and girls of her age would be ashamed of her.

"I'll never have a boyfriend. No boy would come to date a girl who lives in a schoolhouse!" But she was wrong. She was a pretty girl and became quite popular.

Soon after we moved to Ferguson, Genova and Robert divorced and she came back home for awhile. The talk around our house took on a definite feminine quality. In our close quarters, I often overheard conversations of my mother, sisters, girlfriends, and neighbor women. Consequently, I came to understand a woman's point of view better than most men did. I became sympathetic with their feelings, frustrations, and insecurities.

After I entered the ministry, I felt more comfortable around a group of women than did most young preachers. Unfortunately I did not relate as well to men at first, particularly the rough, macho type.

We boys enrolled in Nauvoo Elementary School. For those who finished the eighth grade, the school actually had a graduation service. Most students never went on to high school at that time. I enjoyed school but never expected to go further. I thought I should work full-time on the farms to help support my family.

We assisted the Journeys with their garden. After picking and preparing the vegetables, Mamma canned them on the halves. With his pushmower, I cut Mr. Journey's big yard for 25¢. He would not let me mow it weekly, so the grass got pretty high. I still did not know how to plow, but we chopped cotton and corn in the summer and picked cotton in the fall.

Mr. Journey was an educated country gentleman. I was rather awed by him. He owned no automobile but rode to Dyersburg in an impressive horse-drawn buggy. Sometimes he let me sit on the back. I never recall being invited to sit in the seat alongside him.

After he had read his *Nashville Banner*, he was kind enough to let me come and read sections of my interest. My favorite comic strips were "Dick Tracy," "Flash Gordon," "Gasoline Alley," and "The Katzengammer Kids." Then I turned to the latest reports on how my favorite baseball team, the St. Louis Cardinals, was faring. I was careful to keep the pages of Mr. Journey's paper in proper sequence and to put the paper back where I found it.

Mamma washed and ironed for the Journeys, even though we had no washing machine. Our well furnished only enough water for our use. Delbert and I carried water from a branch some distance away to fill the big iron kettle and wash tubs. I liked to push the clothes up and down on the metal rub board but often rubbed skin off my knuckles. Our method was to soak the clothes, then wash them, and finally boil the white ones.

A wooden punching stick was used to punch them down into the scalding water. Of course, we had no store-bought detergents. Instead we used lye soap that Mamma had made.

Next we carefully lifted the clothes from the black kettle with our punching stick and rinsed them through two or three waters. Sometimes we added bluing to the water. We wrung the clothes out by hand (usually my job as I had a stronger grip than Mamma). We were always proud to see our clothes on the line in the air and sun. They were so clean and smelled so fresh! (Granted, the tedious wash day was not my favorite time of the week.)

After my job was finished, Mamma put the shirts, blouses, and tablecloths in a mixture of water and starch. Ironing was a long, hard job. The irons were heated on our cookstove. The clothes would be sprinkled and placed in baskets ahead of time.

We always had a Jersey cow, which Mamma said was "half our living." While we had no barn, Mr. Journey let us leave her in his at night in exchange for me helping him with his milking. We had a strong leather band around one of the front ankles of our cow. In daytime we attached an iron chain to it and staked her out along the right-of-way of Highway 78. The prolific grass cost us nothing. We boys carried water to her two or three times daily and moved her to a shady spot in the heat of the day.

Old Jersey responded to our kind treatment by giving us about three gallons of rich milk daily. Mamma was most careful with our milk and butter to see that it was the cleanest possible. She aired the empty sorghum buckets a day or two before putting milk in them. Later she skimmed off most of the cream and churned it into fresh buttermilk and butter. Then she worked the water out of the butter until it became quite hard. The cottonseed hulls and meal we fed our cow helped make the butter yellow.

I learned to churn and mold the butter in wooden molds as well as Mamma did. We kept enough butter for ourselves and sold the rest. The Piggly Wiggly store in Dyersburg gladly paid us 50¢ to 75¢ per pound. We put our name inside the wax paper around the butter, and word-of-mouth advertising caused it to sell fast.

Sometimes we swapped butter for groceries. When necessary, we took the money from it to buy cow feed.

As for the buttermilk, Mamma drank a good part of it, since she preferred it to sweet milk. The rest of us drank the skimmed milk, which was healthier for us than whole milk would have been. And sometimes all of us would make a meal on fresh buttermilk and hot cornbread.

At that time we had no refrigerator. With long ropes we let buckets of milk down into our 75-100 feet deep well, keeping them cool and fresh in hot weather.

Once something fell or was thrown into the well that caused the water to taste bad. One bucket at a time, we drew all the water out. Since I was agile, skinny, and lightweight, I persuaded neighboring men to carefully let me down to the bottom of the well to clean it out. Fearing there might be inadequate oxygen or poisonous gas at the bottom, I held a lighted lantern as I rode down on the bucket. It also gave me light for my task.

One day a neighbor proposed to let us have an upright ice box in exchange for some cotton chopping. Genova, Oreathel, and I gladly agreed. Mother feared the ice would be too expensive. To keep it from melting too fast, she kept it wrapped in paper or an old blanket. It did last longer and kept our food cool enough. What a treat when Mamma let us have a piece of the ice for iced tea.

We had no church in the Ferguson community. Soon after moving there I got a ride to the Springhill Baptist Church beyond Nauvoo. I joined that church and was baptized in the Mississippi River. At this simple service, I sensed the Lord was saying "Well done" to me as he did long ago to his Son. Because of the distance and lack of transportation, I seldom was able to go back to Springhill.

Mother caught the vision of doing mission work in our neglected community. So we cleaned and spruced up the vacant room of Ferguson Schoolhouse and invited neighbors in for religious services. (Conveniently, the room had a stage and old pump organ.)

Soon we had several Sunday School classes and preaching services when we could secure a preacher. Once we had a revival and many made professions of faith. To Philemon, Paul spoke of "the church that meets in your home."[14] While not an organized church, we did have regular services at our house.

Oreathel was an "A" student and liked school better than anyone I knew. She had wanted so much to finish high school. But, as she had done many times before, she sacrificed her own preferences for my good.

"A boy needs an education more than a girl," she told me. "You go on and finish high school. I'll drop out and work."

So she accepted the invitation of cousin Birtie McBride to come to Memphis, board with her, and work as a waitress in her cafe, Rainbow Inn. In addition to board, Birtie paid her $7.00 a week, $5.00 of which she sent home to Mamma for our support. Much of what I am I owe to my devoted sister.

Across the road from us the Check Carson family had a farm. They were generous and exceptional neighbors. Mr. Carson put Delbert and me on the same row chopping cotton and told Mamma he would give us 25¢ each per day. (Adult pay was 50¢.) After seeing that we children chopped about as much as grown people, he gave us separate rows and paid us 50¢ each. Soon the daily wage increased to 75¢.

On one occasion the young people of our community were going in Mr. Carson's truck to Reelfoot Lake for an outing. He learned that Delbert and I couldn't go because we didn't have the money to pay for our transportation. Quietly he slipped two half-dollars into Mamma's hand.

"Give these to the boys for their rides and let them go with us," he said. "No one else will have to know."

The Carson children—James, Clyde, Marie, and Betty—were always gracious to us. They were unassuming people who practiced true neighborliness.

One summer Delbert proudly got a job at a sorghum mill.

"I can't pay him," the owner told Mamma, "but I'll give him a gallon of sorghum each day. I sure need that boy if he'll work." And work he did, though only 11 or 12 years of age. Mamma swapped the extra molasses for other food we needed.

Not long before Delbert died in January, 1997, I visited him at his home in Nevada. We reminisced about the early years of our lives.

He smiled and said, "I don't regret we had it hard, L. D. It made use strong!" With that I agreed. Also, I added, "We learned to appreciate everything and take nothing for granted. Even the simplest things."

In the fall we often picked cotton after getting home from school. (A few times I picked by the light of a full moon.) Later in the fall, Mamma and I helped neighbors kill hogs, scald them in a big wooden barrel, and scrape the hairs from their skin. It was customary to eat fresh meat with the family we had helped. At the end of the day they would give us some liver, lights, and hearts (for stew), and occasionally sausage.

At night I studied in the dim light of a coal oil lamp. Then when we could afford it, we bought an Aladdin lamp that was so much brighter. I thought we had come up in the world!

It was such a joy to read by it that Mamma had to fuss at me to get me to come to bed.

Since we had no electricity at that time, our first radio was a Silvertone battery radio from Sears. My favorite programs were "Gene Autry, the Singing Cowboy;" "Roy Rogers;" "The Lone Ranger" (with his faithful Indian sidekick, Tonto); and "Jack Armstrong, the All-American Boy." I thrilled at the sound effects even of ads, such as "Phil-lip Mau-reece." Most were 15-minute programs. At night we laughed along with "Lum and Abner," "Amos and Andy," and "Jam-Up and Honey."

Great radio commentators, such as Gabriel Heater, made the news more exciting. And, of course, on Saturday nights we listened intently to "the Grand Ole Opry."

Another of our simple enjoyments at that time was to go to Dyersburg, sit in someone's car or truck in front of F. W. Woolworth's 5¢ & 10¢ Store, and watch the people go by. We engaged in a lot of speculative character studies.

One day we had a surprise visit from Mrs. Lucy Hart. Tactfully, she handed me a box of used comic books and engaged me in conversation.

"L. D., you do plan to go to high school, don't you?"

"No Ma'am," I replied. "Mamma needs me to work and help make a living."

Then Mrs. Lucy sat down by me and patiently talked some sense into my head.

She explained that when Mamma grew older and could no longer work, she would need my support even more. If I didn't get an education, it would be harder for me to help her. I began to see the reasonableness of her argument.

"But I don't have money to buy school clothes and books," I countered.

She said she would collect some decent used clothes for me from boys who had outgrown them. She would buy my books and I could pay her back by working in her office an hour or two daily after school. That would consist mainly of sweeping the floors, emptying the trash cans, running errands, and answering the telephone.

"But I never did talk on a telephone," I protested. "I don't know how."

"I'll teach you," she assured me.

How grateful I was to Mrs. Lucy for helping me without damaging my self-respect. She let me work for what I got. Like so many others who have crossed my life, she was a great encourager. Young people have a way of becoming what we encourage them to be, not what we nag them to be.

Nauvoo School, grades 7-8. I'm 2nd from left, front row.

Ferguson Schoolhouse where we lived twice.

Poplar Springs Baptist Church (now) where I was ordained.

Chapter 11

Discovering the Power of Words

In the fall of 1938 I enrolled in Dyersburg High School, rated the third best high school in the state. Coming from a variety of little rural schools to a prestigious, city school of about 600 enrollment was a frightening, but challenging, experience. There must have been about 250 freshmen in my class.

The next four years were some of the happiest of my life. I was too small to succeed in high school sports. (According to my old Boy Scout membership card, I weighed less than 95 pounds at the end of my sophomore year.) I was poor and homely, but I was ambitious and determined. Believing God had a worthy purpose for my life, I decided to grasp my opportunities and learn everything I could.

I never felt that my classmates were snobbish or unfriendly toward me. A number of them became my lifelong friends. No one seemed to mind that I lived in a former schoolhouse and wore "hand-me-down" clothes. We don't make friends by feeling sorry for ourselves or resenting the good fortune of others. As Solomon advised, "A man that hath friends must show himself friendly..."[15]

The high school library was our homeroom. I eagerly devoured the books there, one by one. Then someone told me there was a public library where one could check out free books. After locating the building, I turned back twice, thinking it was too good to be true.

At first the librarian would let me take only two books at a time. But when she discovered how rapidly I read, she would let me have six. Wisely, she guided me in the choice of my books. Before I graduated she told me her records showed I had checked out more books than any other of her patrons. I had an insatiable hunger for knowledge and the books were expanding the horizons of my mind and soul.

Some years I at later I wrote a poem about my love affair with words.

When I Read

Words leapfrog in my mind
like frolicking boys at recess.
Sentences dance across my eyes
like smiling skaters traversing ice.
Words shout or whisper to my ears,
calling me to rapt attention.
Phrases, sentences, paragraphs
project motion pictures in my head,
more colorful, active, and exciting
then those upon a movie screen.

—L. D. Kennedy

Competing academically with my classmates from more privileged families was an enjoyable challenge. Out of a senior class of almost 100, I graduated sixth. My gracious classmates voted me "most intellectual boy" of my class that year and elected me Class Poet of '42. (I'm sure this was more compliment than reality.)

My teachers were a constant encouragement to me. Miss Julia Shafer submitted to *Beta Club Journal* a little article entitled "Courage" that I had written as an English assignment. The magazine published it in their April, 1941, issue along with my picture and biographical sketch. This was the first magazine article I ever sold.

Miss Virginia Fields sent to the Memphis *Commercial Appeal* a humorous poem I had written. That paper published my "Tale of the Mouse" in their "Poet's Corner." These surprising successes helped lift my self-esteem and inspired me to write more.

I had already begun publishing poems fairly regularly in the Dyersburg *State Gazette* and was writing news briefs and feature articles for the weekly newspaper. I became a member of the Quill and Scroll and the staff of our school paper, the *Hill Echo.*

The Lord knew I needed to improve my diction and pronunciation, so providentially He led me to become active in the Speech Education Department. Speech, debating, and drama were a great benefit to me, even though no academic credit was given for these activities.

I was fortunate to win trophies and medals for both declamations and debates. In 1942 I received a school letter in Forensics.

During my junior and senior years I worked in the principal's office in my free periods and after school. This prevented me from riding home on the school bus. One afternoon I was caught in a severe thunderstorm. At first I was frightened. Then I heard a sweet song coming from a bird's nest in a big bush near the road.

The courage of the little bird shamed and inspired me. A favorite verse of scripture flashed into my mind: "Fear ye not, therefore, ye are of more value than many sparrows."[16] Mentally I began composing a poem about the lesson I had learned.

Song in a Storm

The sparrow takes some twigs and leaves
And ties them close together;
Then finished in its tiny nest
That sees all sorts of weather.

This fragile house on stormy days
Will sway back to and fro;
But bravely in its humble nest
The bird sings sweet and low.

— L. D. Kennedy

One Sunday afternoon, while Mamma was away visiting, I broke my right arm. I went to the Journey's and called old Dr. Moody. He drove out to Ferguson, examined my arm, and tore off a piece of cardboard from our wood-box to serve as a splint. (It was months later before we were able to pay the kind doctor.)

I had to keep my arm in a sling for about six weeks, and afterward it was awhile before I could use my hand freely. Soon I learned to write with my left hand, so I kept up with my daily lessons and exams. Except my beginning typing course! Not wanting to fail it, I prayed hard and sat in the classes lest I miss needed instructions. As I walked home from school, I mentally typed through my fingers. It worked! Later I made up my exercises and passed the course.

During my junior year I was selected as one of four boys to represent our high school at Tennessee's Boys' State. There we received training in government operations. The local Kiwanis Club sponsored me. They generously outfitted me with a new suit, shirt, tie, shoes, and socks. After that, I was no longer the only boy at DHS in formal club pictures without a suit or coat.

Ms. Mary McWright, my secretarial science teacher, had noticed that I did not eat lunch in the school cafeteria. When she questioned me, I had to admit I could not afford it.

"Would you allow me to fix a sack lunch for you daily and put it in your locker when no one is looking?" she inquired. I agreed.

"What do you I like?" she asked.

"Oh, just anything," I answered.

"Do you like tuna fish?"

"Yes, Ma'am," I assured her, even though I had never tasted tuna fish. So afterwards I unashamedly opened my lunch bag at one of the cafeteria tables and ate delicious, nourishing fruits and sandwiches. Often, I did not know what I was eating, but it was always good.

I deeply appreciated the food but just as much so the fact that my teacher quietly provided it in a way that kept me from losing face with my peers.

Once I had a class with Miss Ruth Gibbons. In response to one of her questions, I boldly used the forbidden word "ain't."

"Don't say that anymore!" she ordered.

"I ain't going to quit saying 'ain't,'" I responded in an uncharacteristic manner. To my surprise, she grabbed me and shook me rather vigorously. I agreed never to say "ain't" again in her classroom.

About my senior year at Union University, Miss Gibbons became librarian of the college. Once she wanted to attend a formal lecture at our finest hotel but had no escort. I volunteered to be her date for the night. It seemed remarkable that she was unashamed to be seen with me. I had a good time. And I didn't say "ain't."

On Saturdays and between school terms I began supplementing our income by working at J.C. Penney's and then the Piggly Wiggly Store. We were now able to move from the schoolhouse to a former store building in South Dyersburg.

Our family became active in the Southside Baptist Church. Hardly any men attended—just a band of faithful women, children, and young people. When I was 17, the church elected me Sunday School superintendent. Besides myself, Edward (Peck) Cooper, who led the singing; Clint Oakley, who taught a Sunday School class; and Willie B. Oakley, who became a deacon—all later were called to preach and became pastors. The labor and prayers of the dear women were not in vain.

One of my spiritual trials came at this time. The Piggly Wiggly Store began asking me to remain at work after midnight on busy Saturdays in the fall. That, to me, was Sunday and violated my conscience. Also, I wanted to be rested for worship and service when I went to church. My pleas and appeals to my manager were of no avail. When he sent me to the store's owner (reputedly an outstanding Christian), I was confident he would understand.

"I thought you said you needed to work," he reminded me.

"Yes, sir, very much so. But not on Sunday."

"Either you work until the manager gives you permission to leave or quit now and pick up your final paycheck." With a heavy heart, that is what I did.

The next week I was on the streets looking for another job. The Black and White Store (now Shainbergs) hired me as stock clerk and promised they would never ask me to work on Sunday. Soon I knew the prices and merchandise better than the longtime clerks. Then the manager gave me a sales book and told me I could start selling.

In accordance with the name of our store, I believed the blacks and whites should be treated with equal fairness and respect. More than once I heard a black woman saying to one of our women clerks: "I want that little white boy to wait on me."

In our store then, we put our sales ticket and money in a cup and pulled a cord to send it up to the office. One Saturday a note from our manager was attached to my cup when it was returned to me.

"Congratulations, L. D., you are leading the store in sales today."

This was so much more exciting than selling bologna and cheese in the back of Piggly Wiggly's. I thanked the Lord that He had honored my decision to obey Him.

Chapter 12

From Sharecropper to Chemical Operator at Oak Ridge

After being introduced to people, they often ask, "Where are you from?" When they see me pause, they don't realize how difficult that is for me to answer. You see, I have lived in at least 44 different places.

Following my graduation from high school we moved to Gibson County to farm. Since World War II was underway, it was difficult to get farm help. So, as green as I was about planting and plowing, Clifford Patterson of Holly Leaf gave me a sharecrop. I knew as much as anybody about chopping and gathering crops, but I did not even know how to harness a team. Clifford almost fell out laughing when I put the collar upside down on the mule.

To feed our soldiers, the War Department requested that more farmers raise sweet potatoes. When I agreed to plant and harvest four acres, I did not know what I was getting into! The plants had to be set out on the row one at a time. For one person to do this the customary way, with a shovel, was a tedious, slow process. Soon I came up with the idea of cutting a V-notch in a broomstick to push the plants into the soft ground.

Since I had set my potatoes so early, they were ready to be harvested in August. This was hot, back-breaking work. Worse than picking cotton. But I must have fed a lot of soldiers.

The following year I bought two old mares and some plow tools. Now I rented instead of sharecropped. Delbert had moved back to Dyersburg and gotten a job at the cotton mill. So all of the crop-work was up to Mamma and me.

We often attended the Pleasant Green Cumberland Presbyterian Church, the only church in our community. However, Mamma and I joined the Poplar Springs Baptist Church, almost four miles south of us. Usually our services were on Saturday nights and Sunday afternoons. Sometimes I walked, and at other times I rode to church on my faithful mare, Dolly.

In the spring of 1944, Mamma married J. E. Richards, a farmer who lived across the creek from us. At the end of that crop year I sold my livestock and tools and went to Ft. Oglethorp, Ga., for induction in the army.

The next day some of us inductees were ordered to strip off all our clothes and walk around naked in front of several doctors. They giggled, as one or two of them pointed at me. I was humiliated! Then they informed me that I could not remain in service, for my feet were too flat.

"I have sold out everything and can't go back to farming," I told them. "What can I do to help out in the war effort?"

"Are you willing to work in a secret operation that will require your leaving home?"

I agreed, but they would not tell me where it was. At their directions I took a train to Knoxville. Late that night a covered army truck transported several of us young men to the Manhattan Project at Oak Ridge, Tennessee.

"Did you have chemistry in high school?" I was asked.

"No," I replied.

"Good!" my interviewer responded. "We'll make a chemical operator of you." The less chemistry we knew the less likelihood there was of our discovering we were working on an atomic bomb.

The Fercleve Corporation where I worked was in a big, black, foreboding building. We were issued gas masks and heavy insulated clothing. The temperature in our building was 115-120 degrees, so lukewarm water bubbled up at numerous locations, and we were given saltpeter tablets. The army threatened us if we told anyone where Oak Ridge was or the nature of our work.

A few days after my arrival someone stole my billfold while I was riding a bus from my barricks to work. The next day I stood at the post office for some time, begging anyone for a 3¢ stamp so I could write home for money. (Our family had no telephone.) For several days I had to beg for food or money to buy some. Most people refused to give me any help at all.

We civilians worked side-by-side with soldiers from the Corp of Engineers. One of these soldiers, who a few days earlier had told me he was an infidel, began buying my meals until a check arrived from home.

My roommate, several years older than I, had been a professor at a church college in Arkansas. He made homosexual advances at me, which I resisted. Then he began ridiculing me for my poverty and ignorance. Seeing me read my Bible daily infuriated him. On occasions he would throw his shoe at me and tell me to "quit reading that old book." He asked questions I could not answer and tried persistently to undermine my faith.

He did succeed in casting some doubts on the reliability of the Bible. This is turn caused me to have doubts about my salvation. My roommate had told me that no one seven years of age could have known what he was doing. Doubts brought torment.

One day I fell on my knees in my room and prayed.

"Lord, I'm not positive I have ever been saved. If not, I want to be right now. What must I do?"

Of course, I knew the way of salvation and had often witnessed to others.

"*I must repent of my sins....* But, Lord, I have repented. Since I was a boy I have repented. Since I was a boy I have hated sin, especially in my own life. I want so much to do your will.

"*I must trust Jesus Christ....* Lord, I have doubted the Bible, but I have never doubted that your Son Jesus paid my sin debt on the cross, rose again, and lives forevermore. For years I have depended upon him as my only hope of salvation. I still do.

"I must love the Lord.... I do love you, Lord, more than anyone. You have been by my side through all the sorrows and hardships of life. Without you I could not live."

A peace flooded my soul and the Lord reassured me. "Don't you see, you are saved. You can't be saved again!"

I arose from my knees, my heart singing, "Blessed assurance, Jesus is mine." Within a few months, I finished reading through the entire Bible. My faith was strengthened and doubts dissolved.

The Lord began impressing upon my heart that he wanted me to preach. I was afraid I had misunderstood him.

"Lord, I'm willing to if you'll just help me know for certain," I told him. But I had no idea how He might go about doing that.

One day I returned to my room and found my Bible opened to Ezekiel 33. Some verses I had underlined weeks before caught my attention:

> "So thou, O son of man, I have set thee a watchman unto the house of Israel; therefore thou shalt hear the word at my mouth, and warn them from me.
>
> "When I say unto the wicked, O wicked man, thou shalt surely die; if thou doest not speak to warn the wicked from his way, that wicked man shall die in his iniquity; but his blood will I require at thine hand.
>
> "Nevertheless, if thou warn the wicked of his way to turn from it; if he do not turn from his way, he shall die in his iniquity, but thou hast delivered thy soul."[17]

Reading this made me tremble. Still I thought that perhaps it was a coincident my Bible was opened there. Whenever I left my room, I closed the Bible. And two more times, soon thereafter, I found it open again to these solemn verses.

"Lord, is this your way of showing me what you want me to do?" I prayed.

"Yes," He answered very clearly, though not in audible words.

Certainly I do not mean to imply that God always calls men to the ministry in such a dramatic fashion. But that was how he called me, and I'm glad.

When the war ended, the Fercleve Corporation invited me to stay on as an employee and transfer to one of their plants in the East. But I knew God had something more important for me.

Back at Poplar Springs Church I arose to share the surprising news of my call with my friends and relatives. But, amazingly, they weren't surprised.

"We've known it all the time," one of them told me. "We just wondered when you'd find it out."

Pastor Kester Cotton set a date for me to preach my first sermon. Actually, I had been working on it for several weeks and was eager to preach. So on September 1, 1945, the dear congregation of my home church listened to my 35-minute message entitled "A Happy and Abundant Life."

But this was the second time I had preached it. The first time was days earlier to a herd of cows resting under shade trees on the backside of Mr. Richard's pasture.

Chapter 13
"Let No Man Despise Thy Youth"

The Poplar Springs Baptist Church licensed me to preach on October 14, 1945. About two months later I enrolled at Union University, a Baptist college in Jackson, Tennessee.

While most ministerial students at that time majored in Bible, I decided to major in English and minor in Bible. This decision, I'm sure, was providential, for years later God led me to become an English professor.

Before I left for college, my pastor said to me, "The way to learn to preach is by preaching." So I preached wherever and whenever I was given an opportunity. This included street services, schoolhouses, cemeteries, and missions of both blacks and whites.

An older ministerial student, Gerald Rowe, was pastor of the First Baptist Church, Savannah. Seeing how much I wanted to preach, he sometimes took me home with him and let me preach at one of his services. I received no pay but was glad to get the experience.

Bro. Rowe told me I should conclude my evening messages and dismiss before 7:30. I was perturbed when I learned the reason. You see, many of his members insisted on being dismissed at that time to attend the Sunday night movie. So the next time, I preached on Elijah calling fire down from heaven and gave a stern warning to those who cared more for worldly pleasures than spiritual matters.

In a few days the Savannah church building burned to the ground. I was never invited by that church to preach again.

On two Sunday afternoons each month Bro. Rowe preached at Turkey Creek, a pastorless church eight miles east of Savannah. Located on a crooked gravel road in the Burnt Church community, Turkey Creek was one of the oldest churches in the Indian Creek Baptist Association. Old minutes of the congregation revealed slaves and whites worshipping together. Bro. Rowe took me with him to the church, introduced me to the congregation, and let me preach for two Sundays.

Then on February 17, 1946 (at the age of 21), the Turkey Creek Baptist Church called me to my first pastorate. A half-time church, it had services the first and third Sundays. On March 10, after a solemn doctrinal examination, the Poplar Springs Baptist Church ordained me to the gospel ministry.

Being young, it seemed most important to me to heed Paul's admonition, "Let no man despise thy youth."[18] So I was sober, zealous, serious-minded, and a bit self-righteous. Looking back on those early years, I'm sure I often took myself and my work too seriously and failed to heed Solomon's admonition, "Do not be overrighteous, neither be overwise...."[19]

Yet my heart was truly set on being a faithful minister and pleasing my Lord. Now that I'm older, I sometimes wonder if I have the depth of love and commitment to Jesus that I had in those younger days.

Fortunately, the association with my delightful members helped to awaken in me a sense of humor.

Once little Clay Jerrolds pulled loose from his mother Opal, ran up to me while I was preaching, pulled at my pants' leg, and called out, "Preachie!" I merely gathered him up in my arms, took him back to his mother, preaching as I went.

Services at our church did not begin at a certain hour by the clock. We started when it seemed enough people were present. Even then, most of the men remained in the church yard, squatting like Indians, spitting tobacco juice, and talking. But when the last song ended before the sermon, they would file in. Several would keep on their hats until I asked them to please remove them.

There were no indoor toilets nor electricity in the homes, but nowhere have I experienced greater hospitality than at Turkey Creek.

"You don't need an invitation," they would tell me. "You are welcome any time."

So I invited myself to different homes weekly. I didn't want them to go to extra trouble preparing for me, and they always had enough for one more. Going from house to house convinced them that I had no favorites. It enabled the families and me to know one another better. I held the babies, played with the children, and teased the teenagers. I knew everyone's name and family.

Late one wintry night, enroute from a revival in Mississippi, my college roommate, Charles Cloyd, and I quietly slipped into the guest bedroom of Jim and Roberta Neill. Like many others they had told me, "Preacher, the latchstring is on the outside." Charles was a bit apprehensive, but I reassured him.

The next morning Jim arose to build a fire in their woodburning kitchen stove. As he glanced through the open doorway to our bedroom, he noticed us. We heard him call to his wife: "Roberta, you'd better fix a little extra this morning. Our preacher's here and he has someone with him."

On a later occasion, Charles and I spent the night with another family. They were gracious but poor people. The dear lady of the house put clean sheets on our bed and was solicitous of our comfort. But after an hour or so we were awakened by the tormenting bites of bed bugs. Not wanting to embarrass the family, we slipped out of bed and lay on the wooden floor until we heard the family stirring next morning. Fortunately, it was summertime so we needed no covering.

The most difficult but delightful character in our church was an elderly gentleman, Hardie Reynolds. Everyone called him Uncle Hard. He wore a black coat and hat and carried a walking stick.

Just across the creek from us stood Turkey Creek Union Church, a Pentecostal congregation. One Sunday morning as I was preaching, a motley-looking little group threw open the front door of our church and marched single file down one aisle toward me. They were led by a large lady with a tambourine, followed by a skinny little man carrying a big guitar. Amazement struck me and I wondered if they had come to take over our service. But our members were smiling and some softly snickering.

Uncle Hard, as so characteristic of him, arose to the occasion. He stuck his walking stick across the aisle, halted the group, and told them: "Go on in front of the pulpit, turn left, go back out the next aisle and to the Union Church across the creek." Most of us were more amused by Uncle Hard's directions than by the actions and appearance of our visitors.

At the front of our auditorium was a wood-burning stove. Uncle Hard would spit tobacco juice at its grate and often miss, spotting the wooden floor or splashing the front where it would sizzle and smell.

My pleas to him to desist went unheeded. Then a plausible plan occurred to me. He had a lovely, neat granddaughter who was the apple of his eye. He would deny to her no reasonable request.

I asked the young lady, with the assistance of her mother, to get a spittoon for Uncle Hard to keep under his pew. She told him she wanted him to spit into it so she would not be embarrassed by his staining the stove or floor.

As expected, Uncle Hard agreed. But unexpectedly, he developed a habit of holding up the neat little spittoon and loudly plunking his chew of tobacco into it.

Grady Hosey was a quiet man whom I admired. In some ways, he reminded me of my own father. Upon arriving in Savannah one Saturday, I decided to locate him and go home with him. Then I was told some shocking news. Just a little while earlier Grady had been eating a cone of ice cream and dropped dead on the street. Rumors as to the cause of his death spread rapidly.

The family asked me to conduct Grady's funeral on Sunday afternoon at Campground Methodist Church, adjacent to the cemetery where he was to be buried. But long before time for the funeral, the little church was over-flowing with people. So the funeral director, from a large funeral home in Memphis, asked me to do the funeral at the graveside in Campground Cemetery. They counted the people coming through the cemetery gate and told me there were about 1,020 — the largest number they had ever had at a funeral.

I was tense, scared, and deeply grieved. When I tried to begin, I completely lost my voice. So the crowd would not see my predicament, I raised my hand signaling for prayer. Being out-of-doors with so many people milling about, they were not puzzled when they could not hear me.

Silently, I began praying earnestly. "Oh, Lord, please give me my voice back. Bro. Grady was a good man and deserves a decent funeral. I'll also share your gospel with this great crowd if you'll let me." In the midst of a sentence of prayer, my voice suddenly returned.

"Thank you Lord!" I exclaimed in relief ... and started preaching.

At this time I had no suit to wear when I preached. Since most of the men wore overalls and jeans, they did not seem to mind. But a few of the ladies thought it would be more appropriate if I had a suit.

I had become quite close to the family of Don and Annie Lee Franks, even though Don was not a church member. Annie Lee digged into a trunk at her house and pulled out the black wool suit Don had worn at their wedding years before. The suit fit me pretty well, so they gave it to me. It was hot in the summer, but my members liked for my sermons to be hot and loud anyway!

September was the month for the annual meetings of Indian Creek Missionary Baptist Association. Messengers from the association's 20 churches gathered for two days of business, reports, missionary promotion, worship, and fellowship.

Excited about attending this big meeting on September 20, 1946, I hitchhiked from Jackson to Savannah. From there I began walking the ten miles or so to the New

Harmony Baptist Church where the meeting was being held. As I plodded down the dusty gravel road, car after car filled with people passed me, throwing dust in my face and upon my black wool suit.

Finally, a kindly Irishman, J. C. Malone, and wife Nell gave me a lift. They were from Cloverdale, Alabama, but liked to go to associational meetings. After the meeting concluded, they volunteered to take me back to Jackson. This was the beginning of a warm, lasting friendship with this dear couple. Mrs. Malone was childless and soon began referring to me as "Son." I knew she loved me like a son.

The annual associational sermon, considered a highlight of the meeting, was scheduled for 11:15 a.m. After the moderator announced that the designated preacher had moved from the association, he called on the alternate.

"No one reminded me, so I'm not prepared," the embarrassed minister responded. Other ministers were invited to bring the message, but all refused.

Uncle Hard had spotted me in the congregation. He stood up, tapped his cane for attention, pointed it at me, and said, "Call on our little preacher. He always has his gun loaded!" I did not wish to embarrass Uncle Hard or the messengers from Turkey Creek, so I preached. The people responded warmly.

During the noon hour, dinner was spread outside. I was approached by people from two or three churches needing a pastor, one for full-time.

For months I had begged my church to let me preach every Sunday, but they had declined. One reason was that they liked to attend the "Decoration Days" held at different cemeteries throughout summertime. These were big social occasions.

After the associational meeting I went back and told Turkey Creek I would leave them unless they agreed for me to preach full-time. They knew I had other places I could go.

"It will cost you no more," I assured them. I just want to preach." They did not want to lose me, so they agreed.

Therefore, in less than a year from the time I was licensed to preach, I was granted the honor of becoming the first full-time pastor in the long history of Turkey Creek Baptist Church.

Turkey Creek Baptist Church, 1948, my first pastorate.

Son Joel and I in front of present Turkey Creek Church.

In revival at Durhamville Church.

Hardie ("Uncle Hard") Reynolds

Chapter 14

Never a Dull Moment

Gerald Rowe soon left Savannah, so I had to hitchhike the 68 miles to and from my church. It usually did not take but a few hours on Saturday mornings from Jackson to Savannah. Frequently I got a ride with someone in a pickup truck on out to Turkey Creek. If not, I walked or rode with someone in a wagon. Many of our members had no other means of transportation in those days.

There was a tall bridge across the Tennessee River. The toll collector was kind enough on Sunday nights to assist me in getting a ride back toward Jackson. I recall one bitter cold night having to ride on the open bed of a rough log truck. I huddled as close to the cab as possible to keep from freezing. Sometimes it was past midnight when I got back to Union University.

While working at Oak Ridge, I had saved over $1,000 to buy a car and had since managed to add some to that.

When Uncle Hard learned of my plans, unbeknown to me he went over the community asking for donations "to help buy the preacher a car." He got 50 cents here, 25 cents there, $1.00 occasionally until he had raised $90, which he proudly presented to me. I knew he meant well and did not want to hurt his feelings, but I was not pleased to have anyone begging on my behalf.

On December 2, 1947, I bought a beautiful brand new, fully-loaded 1947 Chevrolet for $1,811.71. Now my hitch-hiking days were over. Proudly I parked my shiny, black Chevy among the wagons and pickup trucks in front of our church.

It seemed everyone on the creek wanted me to take them to town or for a ride in "our" car. Uncle Hard never let me forget that he and the others had helped me get it. Numerous times I filled it with members and took them to associational activities or even to visit their relatives.

In one family where I visited, a plucky teenage boy had a big festering splinter in one of his fingers. Fearing tetanus, I urged him to let me take him to a doctor in Savannah to get it removed. Being of limited means, he chose an old doctor who was cheap but had a reputation for drinking liquor.

The doctor examined his finger and scrubbed it with antiseptic. He tried to cut the splinter out but his hands were shaking too badly. "You do it!" he ordered as he handed the scalpel to me.

The courageous country boy, who had received nothing for pain, braced himself and told me, "Go ahead." I made an incision over the deeply-embedded splinter and removed it. That day I went home glad I was a preacher and not a doctor.

One Sunday I was preaching on prayer and emphasizing the conditions to answered prayer. I denounced "foxhole religion," or praying only when frightened.

Two rather rough, young ex-servicemen took offense and walked out. Their father stood up and followed them.

So early in my ministry I learned what it was like for people to misunderstand or disagree and seek to embarrass me by getting up during my sermon and tramping out.

Nearly everyone at Turkey Creek seemed to be related in some way. Not only were many of them brothers and sisters or cousins, but a good many were double cousins. Families prided themselves on sticking together.

Once Jamie Reynolds quit attending because he didn't like something I had said or done. On a Saturday soon afterwards I was talking with Jim Neill at the end of a corn row he had just plowed. Suddenly a teenage son of Jamie came trotting up and announced to me:

"Daddy said to tell you he's coming out of the church tomorrow with his family, and what will you have left then?"

"Will he do it? "I asked Jim.

"You bet your bottom dollar he will," Jim replied as he shifted his cud of tobacco.

I was frightened, not wanting to see the first church I pastored experience a split. I went up to the top of the nearby Indian cemetery and prayed.

"Lord, I don't know what to do. Just let me know it's all right and I'll resign and go back to Jackson."

Instead, God laid on my heart a text for a more appropriate sermon than I had planned:

> "And a man's foes shall be those of his own household. He that loveth father or mother more than me is not worthy of me: and he that loveth son or daughter more than me is not worthy of me."[20]

Word of the impending split spread throughout the community. A large, curious crowd was present the following day.

God took over the service and gave me boldness and power I had never before known.

"Does this church belong to Jesus or Bro. Jamie?" I asked them. "Will you follow him or Christ?"

Soon Jamie got up and started walking out. The people looked at him and then at me. I began my invitation.

"If you love Jesus better than anybody and will stay with his church that he purchased with his blood, come give me your hand."

One by one Jamie's family led the way to the front. Among them was his dear wife who had before taken verbal abuse and born him ten children.

"Pray for me, Bro. Kennedy," she begged. "I don't know what he'll do to me, but I must put Jesus first."

Then came Jamie's father Uncle Hard, leaning upon his cane.

"I've always taught our family to stick together, but you've shown us there are times when that's wrong. I'm not leaving the church this time."

Many tears of rejoicing were shed. We sang God's praises. No one else left the church. We covenanted to continue praying for Jamie.

Months later toward the end of our Sunday morning service the front door opened and Jamie came rushing down the aisle toward me. He said he had been home on his knees and gotten right with God.

"I've been like a stubborn billy goat!" he cried. "If you'll take me back and baptize me, I'll make a good member." And we did. And he did.

A later pastor told me that Bro. Jamie remained a cooperative and dedicated member to his death. I have been told that all ten of his children are Christians.

When Turkey Creek called me as pastor, nothing was said about salary. Soon I learned that their custom was to take up offerings on the first and third Sunday mornings and give the pastor about 30 percent. The rest was kept for local expenses and missions.

Some Sundays my part was less than $10, but usually more. According to the associational minutes for 1946, it averaged about $17 each Sunday I preached. If the weather turned bad and no one came, I received nothing.

After we went full-time, our attendance and offerings increased. During 1948 the church gave me $1,029. Average Sunday School attendance was 60. When my percentage of the offerings reached $30 - $50 per week, the church decided it was expedient to put me on a salary!

I learned that when you walk by faith God provides. While I never told my members when I was down to my last dollar, somehow they seemed to know. Many times after a church service or when I visited in a home, someone would slip me some money. They knew my salary was inadequate.

I had never had a high school graduation ring. When Catherine Neill, a young widow, learned I could not afford a college graduation ring, she gave me money and insisted I have one. She was drawing a little monthly pension from the government as her soldier-husband had been killed in World War II.

Once I visited the humble home of a poor young couple with several children. There were holes in walls and floors so big that I noticed cats and even chickens coming through them. One cat climbed upon the table and licked the butter! At their insistence, I had agreed to eat lunch with them. Silently I prayed that the food would not make me sick, ate in faith, but avoided the butter and milk. I knew they were offering me the best they had, and I would never have embarrassed them.

"Bro. Kennedy, you are the first preacher ever to come to our house," the woman told me. Later she pressed a nickel and two pennies into my hand, apologizing because it was all she had. My first impulse was to refuse such a sacrificial gift. But then I remembered the widow's mite, and thanked her.

From the first year of my ministry I began getting invitations to preach in summer revivals. Offerings from them were a helpful supplement to my regular salary.

In the summer of 1947 I received a letter from the Malones, who had given me a ride to the associational meeting the previous year. They had a little country store next to their house.

"We'll move things back and put in some plank seats if you'll come preach for a week in our store," they wrote. "Our community is a mission field. Few of the people ever go to church anywhere. They know little about preachers except those who travel through, setting up a tent or brush arbor and pushing the offerings."

They agreed to keep me in their home for the week but wanted to advertise that no offerings would be taken at the services. I gladly consented. The little store was filled with neighbors, some even sitting in the yard looking through the door. We had a wonderful revival. The spiritual rewards I received were far greater than any monetary offerings would have been. Yet God took care of me in a way wholly unexpected. As I was leaving for home, Mr. J. C. Malone, my godly Presbyterian host for the week, himself gave me $50 and filled my ears with words of warmest appreciation.

When I first went to Turkey Creek, I wanted to take walks into the nearby woods. Some of our men cautioned me against this.

"If you see smoke rising in the woods, it's probably a moonshiner. If you go too close, you might get shot for they don't know you yet." I must confess that at first I had a secret fear I might come upon a "still" operated by one of my members. Thankfully, I never did!

A young couple had moved into our community so the husband could work cutting timber. The wife gave birth to a child that died shortly after birth. They did not attend church anywhere and were very poor. They had no plans for a funeral. I told them I would have charge of it, and it would cost them nothing.

I put the little box casket and parents in my car, drove to the cemetery, and conducted a graveside service. They were grateful.

The following Sunday a deacon handed me $10. He told me that a bootlegger at the edge of the cemetery had observed the proceedings and said, I knew the little preacher didn't get paid anything for that baby's funeral. I want him to have this."

After that, the family of a critically ill or dying moonshiner would sometimes send for me. I considered it an honor that they believed me to be "a friend of sinners."

One family I especially enjoyed visiting was that of Hardin and Kate Neill. The road to their old log house actually ran up the creek for a way. I wanted the Neill children to attend our Vacation Bible School, but Hardin said they couldn't for he needed them to chop his corn. The children were disappointed. Bob Hamblin, a college classmate, was helping me with the Bible School that year.

"Brother Hardin, I want to make a deal with you," I ventured. "Let the children come to the morning Bible School and Bob Hamblin and I will help them chop corn in the afternoons." Hardin agreed, and we enrolled 50 in Bible School that year (1948).

Chopping the corn was no chore for me, but Bob, a city boy, had never done it before. He found the hot sun unpleasant, and the hoe wore blisters on his hands.

"I came to help you in your Vacation Bible School, not to chop corn," he reminded me all week.

At meal time most of the Neill children sat on a long, hewnout, wooden bench. I always insisted on sitting on the bench with them. I also brought many buckets of cold water to their back porch from the spring at the nearby creek.

When Louise and I visited 85-year-old Roberta Neill in 1996, she delightfully related an incident I had long since forgotten. She told how I was staying in the home of Hardin and Kate Neill one day. As I was leaving the yard that afternoon to go visit a sick lady, Kate, who had noticed a small hole in the seat of my pants and a bigger one in one knee, called to me.

"Bro. Kennedy, I know you've got better pants than that! Go back and get you on some others, or they'll think we don't pay you anything."

Dutifully, I obliged. Mrs. Kate loved and respected me as her pastor. But like so many dear ladies around Turkey Creek, she would "mother" me when I needed it.

The way families freely opened their homes to me, shared their food, and loved me like a son has given me a better understanding of what Jesus told his disciples:

> "Verily I say unto you, There is no man that hath left house, or brethren, or sisters, or father, or mother, or wife or children, or lands, for my sake, and the gospel's, But he shall receive an hundredfold now in this time, houses, and brethren, and sisters, and mothers, and children, and lands with persecutions; and in the world to come eternal life."[21]

On winter nights it was a delight to sit around the fireplace with Hardin, watching and listening to the crackling fire. A gentle, older man, he said little. But I felt his love and strength.

A young couple, just recently married, invited me to spend the night with them. They lived in a small frame house with two beds in their combination living/bedroom. Since I was overly modest, I worried about how we would go to bed and arise next morning. It turned out to be right simple. When their backs were turned, I slipped into or out of bed. Then I turned my head toward the wall when they went to bed or got up.

Another thing about that visit I have never forgotten: the skillet of delicious fried corn the young lady prepared for our breakfast. I had never eaten fried corn for breakfast before, but I have a good many times since.

Percy Ray had recommended to some of our men that we get a friend of his from North Carolina as the evangelist for our next revival. They invited him without asking me. He turned out to be a high-pressure evangelist. Especially did he work on the emotions of the little children to get them to come forward.

As the children came to the front, I counseled with them as to why they had come.

"I came because she (or he) did," was the most common response.

Privately I talked with the evangelist about his methods and begged him to let the Holy Spirit do the converting.

We were staying at night in the home of Jim and Roberta Neill and had to sleep together. One night after the rest of us had gone to bed, we heard the evangelist outside by the creek praying at the top of his voice.

"Oh God, the pastor here is keeping us from having revival. Get rid of him or change him," he implored. The sound of his shouting traveled along the creek and through the little valley.

Jim Neill, one of my favorite deacons, came into my room and said, "Bro. Kennedy, I'm going to go 'whup' him!"

"No, Jim," I said. "Just leave him to the Lord." I pretended to be asleep when the evangelist came back to the house and crawled in bed beside me.

The next morning word of this incident had spread over the community. A group of men told me we should close the revival and send him back to North Carolina.

"No," I objected, "it was you who wanted him, so put up with what you've got." From that time, the church never invited another evangelist without my recommendation or approval.

The brother of Jim and Hardin Neill was Dewey. For some time he and I had personality clashes, although later we were reconciled. Frequently, when I went past noon with my sermon, he pulled out his big pocket watch, held it up several seconds, and leisurely observed it. Then after the service he often told me, "Preacher, you sure passed a lot of good stopping places." Of course, now, I realize he was right. I preached too long.

Once Dewey invited a radio quartet from Jackson without consulting me. I had heard reports about them and was not impressed by their spirituality. They sang throughout the Sunday School hour and then announced they would sell songbooks inside the church. I forbade them to do so. Unbeknown to me, word that we were having a "big singing" had circulated throughout the community, and a large crowd had gathered.

At the worship hour, I came to the platform to lead the service. After a bit, Dewey arose and announced:

"We will have a few words from our pastor and then the singing."

But when I got behind the pulpit, I preached, and preached, and preached on Amos 8:10-11. I took as my subject "A Famine of the Hearing of the Word of God." Many, only interested in the singing, got up and left. I supposed it might be my last sermon at Turkey Creek, but most of our members supported me in what I did. Some jokingly referred to it as "the Sunday Bro. Kennedy preached a filibuster."

Several at Turkey Creek thought that to be saved it was necessary to come to the altar, fall upon the mourner's bench, weep, and "pray through." I gave invitations for them to receive Christ right where they were, come forward, and confess him. No one was responding. I felt they were making an idol of the mourner's bench and substituting it for Christ, our true mercy seat.

To stop this, I enlisted one of our young men to help me remove the mourner's bench from the church building.

"No one will be saved now," several of the members lamented, including Dewey.

The church's regular business meetings were each fifth Sunday. There was no preaching on those days. The church had selected a layman as moderator, so they told me I need not come all the way from Jackson for the meetings. They seemed to enjoy giving me second-hand reports of what had transpired.

More than once, the report was: "Bro. Dewey said, 'I make a motion we fire our preacher. We're not having any conversions and the church isn't doing any good.'"

Then I was told that Dewey's quiet, older brother Hardin, would respond: "Sit down, Dewey! You don't know what you're doing."

Still suffered apprehensions about those business meetings. I wondered how long it would be until I was fired.

One of two Friendship Quilts pieced and quilted for me by ladies of Turkey Creek and Mt. Hermon churches.

My graduation picture from Union
University, 1949.

Chapter 15

God's "Mysterious Way"

Uncle Hard's wife, Aunt Mag (as we all called her), was generally considered the most saintly woman in our church. A sweet, old gray-haired lady, she would shout in almost every service. What concerned me even more was that at invitation time she walked around in the church to her grandchildren and implored them to come forward. They loved her and felt they should do whatever she asked.

Several times Aunt Mag began shouting and walking the aisles just as I was getting well into my sermon. Naturally, this distracted me, if not the congregation. I loved and respected her for she was a dear tenderhearted soul who cared about others. Yet I believed the biblical admonition that in the church one should speak at a time.

Never wanting to embarrass Aunt Mag publicly, I went to her house privately and reasoned with her from the Scriptures. She did not appear offended and agreed to refrain from shouting while I was preaching. After a few services, I heard statements such as, "Aunt Mag has lost her power."

So at a convenient time in one of the services I exclaimed, "Aunt Mag has not lost her power. She has more power than she has ever had." She looked at me and smiled. Our friendship grew.

While attending a Bible Institute in Marion, Kentucky, I had met a great preacher and singer named Buell H. Kazee. He was pastor of the First Baptist Church in the college town of Morehead, Kentucky. Later I wrote and invited him to come hold a two-weeks' revival in August, 1948, at Turkey Creek. I felt he was just the one we needed to counteract the over-emotionalism still cherished by many in our congregation.

I leveled with Kazee about the poverty of most of our people and the backwardness of our community.

"You can't expect much pay," I told him, "but we need you."

He agreed to come. Later he told me he bought a round-trip ticket to Nashville, where I met him. He supposed he might not get a large enough honorarium to buy a return ticket. But, to his surprise, Turkey Creek gave him a generous offering.

We had morning and evening services. Bro. Kazee brought great solos and deeply spiritual preaching such as our church had never heard. In their homes, families sometimes persuaded him to pick up his banjo, play, and sing the genuine old folk songs for which he was famous when he was a Brunswick recording artist of the late '20s. Though a city preacher, he certainly related to our country people.

That week Kazee and I stayed in the home of a dedicated young couple who had never obtained modern conveniences. But they freely shared with us the best they had.

For grooming or bathing, we had cold water from the spring. We had just one washcloth between us, so we kept it washed out well. Kazee was not perturbed by the inconveniences. He taught me how to shave with cold water by first cleansing my face well. Little did I think that I would be able to help him just as much that week.

In conversations he shared with me that he had been working on a book manuscript but didn't know how to get it published. Since I was an English major and had studied creative writing, he asked my advice. I told him acceptable manuscript conventions and suggested a few potential publishers. I stressed that he should send his manuscript to only one publisher at a time.

Not optimistic about anyone wanting to publish his book, he sent copies to two publishers. Soon he wrote me an urgent letter.

"What can I do, L. D.? Both publishers have agreed to publish my book!" With my advice, he got the matter cleared up. In 1951 Wm. B. Eerdmans Publishing Company published his book under the title *Faith is the Victory*. Since then it has been reprinted numerous times and has become a sort of spiritual classic. Before then, however, a lot of its chapters were preached at our humble little country church!

Since I received no financial assistance from my family, my regular preaching income was not enough to pay for college tuition, books, fees, and automobile expenses. (Of course, I wasn't the only student having a difficult time. Once I caught my roommate trying to squeeze toothpaste from my tube to his!)

In the fall I tried to schedule my classes during the mornings. Other students did not know that I kept a cotton sack and work clothes in the back of my car. I would leave campus at noon and drive to the country. At a thicket I would change into my work clothes and seek out a cotton patch. Wages were better than in the '30s, and I knew how to pick cotton.

One day, in discouragement I climbed to the top of the old Indian cemetery, sat on a beech stump, and poured out my heart to God.

"Lord, I thought when you got me, you were getting a preacher. But you got a dud. I'm a failure. I preach with all my heart, but people aren't being converted. Some of the folks are tired of me and would like to see me leave. I try to counsel with families who are having problems, but things often get worse. I'm not wise enough to pastor these people.

"I don't know how I'm going to meet my school expenses. I've got a painful ulcer from worrying. Just let me quit, go back home, and farm.

"I've tried hard, but I've learned I can't do anything myself. I surrender my ministry back to you. If anything ever comes of it, you'll have to do it. I am a most unprofitable vessel."

No robed choir was singing. No organ was playing soft music. But suddenly something happened to me. I passed over Jordan! I do not mean I was saved again, but my old self was crucified afresh, and I just yielded myself to God to do with as He pleased.

Sweet peace flooded my soul.

One Sunday morning I preached on "The Touch of Faith," and Hazel, the 12-year-old daughter of Dewey and Neely Neill came forward to confess Christ. Her parents rejoiced and admitted to me that she was saved indeed without the mourner's bench. (When I visited at Turkey Creek in August of 1995, Hazel came to me, identified herself, and told how Jesus was still precious to her.)

I began seeing that what I could not do, God could do. He began saving souls and doing many wonderful things for our church. Differences were resolved and my friendship with Dewey Neill and his family grew. They even drove a distance to visit me after I left my pastorate there.

The creek alongside our church building served as our baptistry. Some converts insisted on baptism in March or April. They recounted stories of relatives who claimed they broke the ice to be baptized. But even in the summertime it was a trip of faith to step into the cold, cold spring-fed waters of Turkey Creek. Yet none of us ever caught a cold from it.

Almost every Sunday some kind lady filled a pitcher from the spring and set it and a glass on one side of my pulpit. I'm afraid those refreshing sips between points only encouraged me to preach longer.

Just before I began preaching at Turkey Creek, a young Methodist girl from our community, Frances Neill, married Lauren Locke, a Baptist boy from Mississippi. They then lived in the house with Frances' parents, Ulvie and Mary Neill.

The Lockes and Neills attended services at Turkey Creek rather regularly, and I visited in their home as though they were members. Mrs. Mary was a great cook. Her chess pies were the best I ever ate. They must have contained at least six or seven eggs. Sometimes she sent me back to Jackson with two or three freshly baked pies and all of the eggs her hens laid on Sunday.

Since Lauren was less than two years older than I, it was fun to visit with this family. On Saturday afternoon he and I would take soap and towels and go bathe in the creek. We also engaged in waterfights in the cold rocky stream. Recently Lauren recalled an incident I had forgotten.

"When you pulled off your undershirt, it had several large holes in it. You slung it down the creek, declaring, 'I know I can do better than that.'"

Then tragedy struck in the home of my friends. Frances gave birth to a severely afflicted daughter, Judy, who had a large pouch with brain cells outside her lower skull (called minengocele or hydrocele, I believe). The family were distraught. Local doctors said nothing could be done for her and she would live for a few days at the most.

I called the Baptist Hospital in Memphis and they mercifully agreed to admit Judy. As Lauren carefully cradled the infant in his arms, I drove the long trip to the hospital. A South American surgeon, Dr. Fairman, performed surgery on Judy. After a month in the hospital she was brought home for awhile. Then she was taken back for another month of treatments.

Judy has always had a special affection for me, for when she was but a child her parents told her I saved her life. Of course, I did not. That was a miracle of God.

This sobering experience had a profound effect upon Lauren and Frances. They began tithing and searching the Scriptures. Lauren soon felt a call to the ministry. In August of 1952 he preached his first sermon at Turkey Creek Baptist Church. Since then he completed college and has had several successful pastorates in his home area.

On August 13, 1995, we surprised Lauren and Frances by appearing at their 50th anniversary celebration. Judy spotted us before we entered the building. Loyal, lifelong friends like these are one of the greatest rewards of one's ministry.

For some time I had been urging the church to build needed Sunday School rooms, but the men were busy with their own work. Tom Jerrolds offered to donate timber and cut it up into lumber at his sawmill. Mancil and Maxell Neill, two young men about my age, and I went to the woods and cut the needed trees. The lumber was stacked behind the church.

On August 17, 1947, plans for a Sunday School addition on the back of the church were approved. Work proceeded slowly, however.

That year I spent my Christmas vacation working on the building. One day I was performing the lonely task of putting up strips of weatherboarding by myself when Hundley Jerrolds came to the spring for a bucket of water. He walked over to me and engaged me in conversation concerning some of my recent preaching on the grace of God. I clarified points and answered his questions. Then he slowly turned and proceeded home.

After graduating from seminary, I led revival services at Turkey Creek. It was a joy to see Hundley again, for this big generous man had always been one of my staunchest supporters.

"Preacher, I've got something to tell you that may surprise you," Hundley said. "Remember that Christmas you were weatherboarding the church and I had a talk with you? Well, I was saved during that conversation! I didn't tell the church or ask for baptism again for a long time. I had been a member and deacon so long I just didn't know how people would take it."

I marveled at what he told me. Like the Samaritan woman in John 4, Hundley came to the spring for water and returned home with living water. Furthermore, I was God's instrument that day in a work much more important than weatherboarding the church.

William Cowper was so right when he wrote in one of his hymns, "God moves in a mysterious way/His wonders to perform...."

At one of our associational meetings I had censored my alma mater for maintaining social fraternities and sororities. I felt their sometimes snobbish, exclusive attitudes were unChristlike. Dr. Warren F. Jones, president of Union University, was at the meeting and doubtless embarrassed and displeased by my report. We had other differences later. Once he called me to his office and threatened my expulsion from college.

Awhile later his brilliant wife, Dr. Dixie Markham Jones, one of my professors, called me to her office and inquired what I had done that upset her husband.

"L. D., as long as I'm his wife, he'll not expel you from college," she promised.

Years later I learned it was Dr. Warren F. Jones who had recommended me to the faculty of Campbellsville College, where he had been president before coming to Union University. This gracious man had forgiven what he considered my youthful impulsiveness.

For some time I had a vision of starting a mission on Highway 64. In 1948 a former store building became vacant after the owner had lost his beer license. I contacted him about renting the building so we could hold Sunday afternoon mission services. He agreed but said it would be rent free and he would pay the light bills.

Turkey Creek members came over, cleaned the walls, scrubbed and disinfected the floors. We made rough seats by nailing planks onto wooden blocks.

Soon after opening the mission we obtained permission to hold services in the vacant building of Mt. Hermon Cumberland Presbyterian Church. I conducted a revival and attendance at our afternoon services grew. The large one-room building, almost 100 years old, was lighted by Aladdin lamps and heated by a pot-bellied wood stove. Sometimes in cold weather I had to preach with my overcoat on.

The ladies of the mission pieced a Friendship Quilt for me with their individual names in each block. Then they gathered at the mission and quilted it. I still have this treasured reminder of their love and kindness.

One of the boys, about 12, who walked to the mission services was Hardin Hosey, whose family were Methodists. Before long he made a profession of faith. Later, unbeknown to me at the time, he became a Baptist and answered the call to the ministry.

Years later, while he was a student at Southern Baptist Theological Seminary, Hardin looked me up at Campbellsville, Kentucky. I learned that he had married Betty, a sister of Bro. Lauren Locke. Presently he pastors near Marion, Kentucky.

Out of the Mr. Hermon Mission was born the Mount Hermon Baptist Church on October 14, 1951. Now it is a thriving congregation with over 300 members. It was my privilege on October 8, 1995, to preach the homecoming message for their 44th anniversary.

Turkey Creek may have been a small, remote church, but it has had a powerful spiritual influence on the lives of many people—including myself. The simple God-fearing people there taught me a lot about humility, patience, perseverance, and forbearance. They were my "first love" so far as churches are concerned. They will always be dear to my heart. I remained their pastor until September, 1949.

On February 18, 1996, the church invited me back to commemorate my 50th year in the ministry. They now have a considerably larger modern brick building with lovely padded pews and stately matching pulpit furniture. A spacious baptistry stands back of the choir. It appears they have a capable pastor and progressive program. God has done great things for them.

On May 24, 1949, I graduated from Union University. It took me just three and one-half years, even though I was pastor of a growing church. Perhaps the greatest miracle was that through God's provision, I paid all my college bills and graduated debt-free.

During my years at Union I had three unique, but delightful, roommates. Charles H. Melton was physically blind but brilliant and competent. He taught me that handicaps are not so much physical as attitudinal.

Charles had been dating a young lady from Lambuth College, across town. Every step, street, and lamppost enroute to Lambuth was stamped into his mind. Once he persuaded me to go with him on a double date. About halfway back to Union University we encountered a rainstorm and power outage. As I grappled in the dark, he chuckled, "Take hold of my arm, you blind cuck, and I'll lead you safely home." And, amazingly, he did! Afterwards Charles earned a doctor of education degree from Southwestern Baptist Theological Seminary and later served as professor of religion at Mississippi's Clarke College.

Charles Cloyd, fresh from the corn fields of Western Kentucky, was small in stature, big with words, and lacking in social graces. He was a non-conformist who enjoyed arguing especially about theology. At that time, he was unpopular on campus, and I did not want him for a roommate. But he was persistent. I literally threw him out of my dormitory room and locked the door. Later I looked up and saw him crawling through the transom, his big eyes gazing pleadingly at me. Finally, I let him in.

Soon I discovered he was as brilliant as my first roommate. Deeply versed in the Scriptures, he challenged many of my traditional views. As we discussed or debated, each of us developed a deeper and more balanced understanding of spiritual truths. Soon he became and has remained one of my most loyal friends. From the experiences with him, I have learned the danger of judging from first impressions.

For many years now, Charles has been a professor at Mid-Continent Baptist College in Mayfield, Kentucky.

George E. Clark, my third roommate, was a pleasant dreamer who could sometimes be found on the dormitory roof looking at the stars and quoting poetry. Like the other roommates, he was a ministerial student. Unlike Cloyd, he would sometimes agree just to keep from arguing. George later earned a doctor of philosophy degree. He returned to his alma mater, became professor of English and chairman of his department until his retirement.

Little did any of us four roommates dream at that time that all of us would become college professors as well as preachers.

Under the tutelage of good English teachers, my interest in creative writing blossomed in college. Frequently I submitted poems to our college newspaper. In 1949 I represented Union University at the Southern Literary Festival held at the University of Mississippi. Competing in another literary festival, I won first prize in poetry for a sonnet sequence entitled "Love Lyrics to Lauraleen." During graduation week I won the annual M. E. Dodd Expository Writing Contest, for which I was awarded a set of B. H. Carroll's *Commentaries*. This essay was published in August, 1951, as the lead article in *Home Life* magazine.

Chapter 16

"Enlarge the Place of Thy Tent"

In the fall of 1949 two churches called me as pastor: Cloverport (near Boliver) and Macedonia (near Ripley). I accepted the call of Macedonia. It was a larger church and had a pastorium which I needed, because I was engaged to be married. I moved on the field and agreed to their salary of $40 per week.

Cloverport, however, would not accept "no" for an answer. They told me they had called me unanimously and that I must have misinterpreted the will of God. Soon I learned that they had a large unpicked cotton patch, the income from which was to be used to install gas heat in their little concrete block auditorium. But they had no one to lead them in getting their job done.

I agreed to preach for them awhile on Saturday nights and Sunday afternoons. One week I announced that I would stay over until Monday and help them pick their cotton.

"I'll be in the field early, and I want all of you to be there, too," I said. I will pick more cotton than anyone else who comes. I dare any person in this community to make me out a liar." This friendly boast I made to arouse interest and promote the project.

The next day there was a field full of pickers. Buddy Laney, said to be the best picker in the community, took a row by the side of mine. This wiry, red-haired man was not a church member. He planned to make me eat my words and embarrass the preacher before his congregation.

When I went to the scales to weigh, Buddy went. Sometimes he had a pound or two more than I. At other times I had the most. Our fierce race was the talk of the field. Thankfully, at the end of the day I had picked a few pounds more than Buddy. His respect for me increased, and we became good friends.

Not long after that Cloverport Church got its heating system installed. Though small, it has been an active church. Several ministers have been ordained from its membership.

While Macedonia Church voted on me as pastor, I remained outside the building. Then they sent for me to come back inside and told me I had received a unanimous call. But as the members came by to greet me, Talmage Crihfield, who was a deacon and Sunday School superintendent, made a frank acknowledgement to me.

"Preacher, I want to tell you something before you hear it from someone else. I didn't vote for you the first time. Not that I have anything against you personally, but I just wasn't sure you're the right man for the job. But when I saw everyone else wanted you, I asked that another vote be taken and I made it unanimous. If you'll forgive me, I'll work with you and support you wholeheartedly."

"There's nothing to forgive," I assured him. "I admire any man who stands for his convictions. I'll hold nothing against you."

This dear man was true to his promise. He supported me, prayed for me, and encouraged me. To this day he is like a flesh-and-blood brother to me.

In November, 1949, Charlene Traver and I were married. In 1951, Silvia, a lovely little daughter was born to us. No father was ever prouder.

The church bought an old used mimeograph machine for $50. I wrote and typed each issue, hand-cranking out 200 copies of "The Macedonia Messenger," to be mailed to members and prospects. Then I folded and addressed each one of the newsletters. Since I had no secretary, this job took considerable time, but I knew it would be worth the effort. An informed church membership will attend and give better.

Our offerings began increasing after members read the treasurer's reports in the newsletter. Some remarked they never before had any idea how much it cost to run a church. Sometimes we used the "Messenger" to raise money for medicines or to pay hospital costs of indigent members. After I printed sermon summaries and promoted upcoming sermons, attendance grew.

The church initiated a weekly radio program, county home services, a discipline program, and sick and needy fund. At the cost of almost half our annual receipts, we raised money to purchase beautiful new pews, pulpit furniture, and 24 choir seats. Best of all we saw lives redeemed, transformed, and added to our church.

A highlight of my ministry occurred in 1951. Dr. T. T. Shields, pastor of the Jarvis Street Baptist Church, Toronto, Canada, invited me to come visit him for a week in June and preach in his church on Sunday morning. Often called "the Spurgeon of Canada," Dr. Shields pastored this historic church for about half a century.

When I arrived, Dr. Shields escorted me to the stately Fortnac Arms Hotel, where the church had reserved, not a room, but a suite for me! Part of the time Dr. and Mrs. Shields entertained me in their home.

On Sunday morning I preached to the dedicated congregation at the Jarvis Street Baptist Church. The Gothic architecture of this spacious, lofty auditorium was awe-inspiring.

Before I preached Dr. Shields took me into his study, prayed for me, and insisted: "When you arise to speak, say nothing about me. Just exalt the Lord and proclaim his word."

When I looked out over the great congregation in the auditorium and balconies, I was almost overwhelmed by my unworthiness and inadequacy. Standing behind the pulpit, about eight feet wide, from which Dr. Shields had preached for more than 40 years, was a memorable experience for this country preacher. I could never have imagined that the Lord would have taken me that far from the cotton fields of my youth. But the Lord strengthened me as I took my thoughts off myself and the historic church. I preached with joy, and the people responded warmly.

As I dealt with more complex church programs and organizations, I began to realize I needed seminary training. So I applied for admission to the January, 1952, term of Southwestern Baptist Theological Seminary in Fort Worth. I resigned my pastorate in September to take my family to Oregon to visit relatives before proceeding to Texas.

While in Oregon I worked as a lumber puller at the Coos Bay Lumber Company, the largest lumber mill in the world. Soon it came to the attention of the management that I was a responsible college graduate. I turned down a lucrative offer from the company president to become his own personal secretary and accompany him on business trips to various countries.

The First Baptist Church (American Baptist) of Coos Bay was pastorless. I began preaching for them. They were a warm, gracious people. Soon they inquired if I would consider becoming their pastor. They said the fact I was Southern Baptist made no difference to them. However, I declined for God was leading me to seminary.

After a Sunday morning service, I was greeting members of the Coos Bay congregation as they departed. My eyes were drawn to a plainly-dressed young couple I had not seen before. They told me they were Ed and Eleanor Jones, salmon fishermen from Ketchikan, Alaska. They had docked their boat nearby and were visiting. The response they gave to the service and my preaching was most encouraging.

A few days later the Joneses called and requested an appointment to see me for several hours. Inwardly I groaned, thinking they probably were wanting marital counseling. But I was amazed at their request.

"We want you to teach us the Bible," Eleanor said. "We've gone to church before but never heard the gospel until a few months ago. We were both saved but never heard any more true Biblical preaching until we heard you. In our fishing boat at night we have been reading the Bible. But there is so much we don't understand."

"What in the Bible do you want to know about?" I asked.

"Everything," they replied. "Just start at the beginning."

Never before in the years of my ministry had anyone made such a request of me. How could I teach the whole Bible in a few hours? But this young couple were in earnest.

Breathing a prayer to God for help, I started with the creation in Genesis, pointing out the most significant Biblical events as I continued. Especially did I emphasize the major doctrines and themes (such as redemption) that ran through both testaments.

The joy and excitement of my audience of two were unbelievable. At various times I suggested that we should stop if they were growing weary. But they begged me to continue. About midnight I finished.

With tears of joy Ed and Eleanor embraced me and one another. Then Ed addressed his wife.

"Do you have the check made out?"

"You don't have to pay me a thing for what I have done," I protested. "Sharing God's word with you tonight has been one of the greatest blessings of my life."

"But we aren't paying you," Eleanor said. "Last week each of us was in a separate room praying about where to give our next offering. We received answers and met again in the living room. At exactly the same time we each said, 'Reverend Kennedy.'"

After they left, I opened their check and could not believe my eyes. It was for $400! Through this humble couple, strangers to me until just recently, God had provided the means for my seminary books, matriculation fee, and living expenses until I could find a part-time job.

Ed and Eleanor sent further gifts to me at the most strategic times while I pursued my seminary studies. I never wrote them about being in need, but they were so close to the Lord that they sensed it and obeyed. Without their help I do not see how I could have remained in seminary. The remarkable thing about their support of me was they were not my relatives, not Southern Baptists, and had never heard me preach but a few times. But their spiritual sensitivity was extraordinary.

The seminary classes were exciting, inspiring, and mind-stretching. My professors were knowledgeable and devout. Dr. T. B. Maston, professor of social ethics, was probably the greatest teacher I ever had. Dr. Cal Guy, professor of missions, made world missions come alive.

In Greek, no one surpassed Dr. Curtis Vaughan, who became a dear personal friend. (On one occasion when he was away in revival, I took his wife to the hospital for the birth of their child. I smiled when a nurse addressed me as Dr. Vaughan.)

My New Testament professors were Dr. Ray Summers and Dr. J. W. Mac Gorman. Nothing dull about their classes! Dr. James Leo Garrett, professor of theology, was brilliant. Many declared he remembered the names of every one of the students who had ever been in his classes.

I never realized the value of philosophy until I took courses under Dr. John Newport, professor of philosophy of religion. Finally, I learned most of what I know about church administration and religious education under Dr. J. M. Price. Of course, there were other great professors but these stand out in my mind.

Unfortunately, not everything during seminary days was joyful. An unexpected tragedy struck my family, too painful for me to recount. Filled with sorrow and grief, I was left alone with my little daughter Silvia. Juggling my schedule of classes, work and caring for Silvia (including arranging for babysitters) was a heavy task, but by the grace of God I survived.

Usually I was able to schedule my seminary classes during the mornings of Tuesday through Friday. I needed a part-time job badly. The employment office sent me to the Dorsey Grain Company, probably the oldest grain brokerage in Texas.

After interviewing me and checking my typing skills, the company offered me a full-time secretarial job, which, of course, I could not take. Then I persuaded them to let me work part-time at an hourly rate until they secured a regular worker.

When prospects came by for interviews, I prayed as I typed dictation from a wire recorder: "Lord, please don't let them hire unless he needs the job worse than I."

Meanwhile, Mr. James A. Dacus, the vice-president, marveled that I was completing daily all the required secretarial work.

"You don't have to work that hard," he said. "You're doing as much as we would expect of a full-time employee."

"Then please let me have the job," I begged. I like to work at this pace. I can keep it up."

After a few days they gave me the position. Mr. Dacus and Mrs. Dorsey, the owner of the company, became like family to me. They taught me so much about public relations, administration, and running a big business.

In the years following, these insights proved extremely valuable as I used them in the responsible business management of my pastorates. Members frequently remarked that I knew more about money management than any pastor they had had. These skills also served me well when I became a department chairman at Campbellsville College. If we are surrendered to God, He is always preparing us in advance for future responsibilities.

Most of the time I was in seminary I pastored the Post Oak Baptist Church, about 150 miles northeast of Fort Worth. It was located in a drought-stricken rural community. They agreed to pay me $40 per week. My actual remunerations amounted to $17 a week, just about enough to cover my round-trip automobile expenses. But that did not bother me, for I wanted to preach so badly, and I knew the people were poor.

Silvia and I enjoyed being together on the drives to Post Oak. In the summertime I would stop and get us cold mugs of root beer. Then we would laugh at each other as we burped. Once I heard her tell some members, "Daddy got me a beer today." I smiled, confident they knew this was a child talking.

Several years later the Post Oak Church disbanded. They were discussing what to do with the money left in their treasury. The treasurer revealed to them that they still owed me a considerable amount. Imagine our surprise when we opened the letter and found a $700 check from Post Oak Church. It came at a time when it was greatly needed.

I completed my three-year seminary program in two and one-half years, earning the bachelor of divinity degree. I was exhausted physically, mentally, and emotionally, and uncertain about the future.

The Dorsey Grain Company offered me a good full-time position if I would remain with them. But I did not care about making money. I just wanted to preach the Good News and minister to others.

About that time Talmage Chrihfield telephoned me.

"Preacher, I'm on the pulpit committee of Macedonia Church. We want you to come back as our pastor and take up the work you left off when you went to seminary. We don't believe your job is finished."

"I have one question to ask you, Talmage," I teased. "Will you vote for me this time?"

"You know I will!" he assured me.

So from January 2, 1955, to August 20, 1958, I had the honor of pastoring Macedonia Baptist Church for the second time.

Macedonia Baptist Church, Ripley, TN.

First Baptist Church, Maury City, TN.

Delbert, Oreathel, L.D. and Genova.

Chapter 17

A Mission-Centered Ministry

When I returned to Macedonia, I outlined to the church my four main objectives. By God's enabling, I wanted to build: (1) a spiritual church, (2) a stewardship church, (3) an evangelistic church, and (4) a missionary church. We began intensive training sessions for Sunday School teachers and started a Deacon Family Ministry Plan.

Soon it became obvious that we needed more Sunday School space. Mostly by hand with picks and shovels we dug a full basement under the church in which we constructed Sunday School rooms, assembly rooms, and a kitchen.

Next we took a religious census of our community and set up enrollment and prospect files. Two or three of us regularly drove down little dirt and gravel roads, bringing people to church. Some of today's leaders in the church were little children we brought to Sunday School and Vacation Bible School.

Radio Station WTRB, Ripley, offered me a prime slot for a radio program, 1:30 - 2:00 p.m. on Sundays. But they stipulated I must come in person or record the services on high fidelity equipment. I requested the church to buy a high fidelity R.C.A. tape recorder for this purpose. They said they could not afford it at the time. So sure was I that it was God's will that I announced, "I'm going to Memphis Saturday and buy the recorder myself. I don't have the money, but the Lord will provide."

Unbeknown to me, the Lord had already directed Ed and Eleanor Jones in Oregon to send me some money. Accompanying their check, which arrived before Saturday, was a little note.

"God has laid it upon our hearts that you have a special need at this time. Use this check for that purpose." Almost to the dollar, it paid for the powerful recorder I needed plus tapes and two loudspeakers that we used with it for a public address system in our church auditorium.

Our radio program was called "The Abundant Life Broadcast." Some weeks I also recorded daily messages for "The Pastor's Study," which were aired at 10:30 a.m. The radio station was pleased with the quality of my tapes.

Next we began a tape ministry for the sick and shut-ins of our community. None of them had televisions then, so they were delighted that we brought our services to their homes.

Racial tensions in the South were high in the mid-'50s. At my church and on my radio program, I sometimes spoke out against racial prejudice and injustices. I emphasized that Christianity is love and that Christ as our Saviour and example crossed over all racial and color lines. I reminded the hearers that God is no respecter of persons.

Some in my radio audience were angered by my views (or what they had heard second-handed). By anonymous letters and telephone calls they threatened to burn my house down and ride me out of the community on a rail unless I shut up. When their threats went unheeded, they pressured my members to fire me. Even though many of my members themselves had prejudices against blacks, they stood up for me as a servant of God who had a right and responsibility to preach the Word as I understood it. Never was I more proud of Macedonia Church!

I had sent an article dealing with the sin of racial prejudice to several magazines. Instead of mere rejection slips, the editors wrote me apologetically that while they agreed with me, the article was "too hot to handle."

Then editor John Caylor published it as the lead article in the May, 1955, issue of *Home Missions*. Beautifully illustrated by the magazine, the article was titled "The Christian Policy Toward Other Races." In it I advocated two clear Biblical principles: (1) "that we should respect all people as being of equal worth before God as ourselves" and (2) "that we should treat members of other races as we ourselves would like to be treated."[22]

John Caylor wrote me that he received letters of commendation of my article. He also received some nasty letters for publishing it and threats to get him fired. But he stood his ground on Biblical principles even though a few readers cancelled their subscriptions.

I was further gratified when Miss Edwina Robinson, executive secretary of the Women's Mission Union of Mississippi wrote me on May 5, 1955, and requested permission to use a great deal of the material in my *Home Missions* article in their State Mission Week of Prayer. Of course, I consented.

Actually, I received almost no negative letters from those who read my article. Instead, I received a number of letters from people in different states of the Southern Baptist Convention agreeing with me and thanking me for writing the article.

November 11, 1956, is a memorable day. Louise Newman and I were married at Macedonia Church before a church-full of well-wishers. Since my salary was just $60 a week, I did not know how far we could go for a honeymoon. But as we were leaving the church, Talmage Crihfield slipped me a $100 bill. We had a great honeymoon in the Smoky Mountains.

Louise was making more money than I. She immediately quit her job to stay home with Silvia and help me in my ministry. In November, 1957, our first son, Mark, was born. A father's first son is someone special!

Louise and I had sometimes talked about doing direct mission work. Troy Brooks, a home missionary for three western states, appealed to us to come assist him in a 10-day Vacation Bible School. My friend Robert Emerson and I agreed to go during our summer vacations, with our families, and take Christ to Clarksdale, Arizona. This town had no evangelical church.

The three Emersons and we Kennedys left in my 1955 Chevrolet in June, 1958. We were loaded to the hilt.

Rather late the third night we arrived in Clarksdale. But to our dismay Bro. Brooks did not meet us. We learned that he had been critically injured in a car accident as he was enroute to get other workers to help us in the Bible School. So we were on our own among strangers in a strange city. At least we did find the vacant house to stay in that Bro. Brooks had rented for us. Being short on money, we had to rely heavily on dry soup beans, potatoes, and corn bread.

We held our school in the American Legion Hall of Clarksdale. Over 60 children attended, about half of whom were Indians. There were also Mormons, Catholics, Church of Jesus Name, Protestants, and unchurched. There was still a great deal of reserve on the part of the Indians as this was their first year to be integrated with whites at public school or V.B.S.

The Indians especially enjoyed action songs and activity. We had no money for any craft supplies. So during the handicraft periods we played baseball with both boys and girls. They seemed to enjoy that immensely.

One little boy couldn't find Genesis or Matthew in the Bible another child loaned him. I showed him how to locate books of the Bible, and he was so thrilled upon finding Leviticus. Later I spoke of the crucifixion of Christ.

"Who killed him?" he asked with evident concern. I eagerly grasped this opportunity to explain to all the children the atoning death of Christ for us sinners. During the school, there were a number of professions of faith.

We had commencement for our V.B.S. on the night of June 27. The next day we headed home, hoping and praying our few dollars would be enough to get us there. And God was so faithful! When we pulled into our home driveway, I had less than one dollar, and the gasoline tank was nearly empty.

Things were going well at Macedonia. By October, 1957, our little church had a Sunday School enrollment of 210. Many members, including every deacon and deacon's wife, had pledged to tithe. Mission offerings were mushrooming. Best of all, people were being saved and added to the church.

"You taught me the joy of giving," was a cherished tribute from one of my deacons during my last service at Macedonia. Considering the liberal increase in weekly offerings and missionary giving, I believe many other members might have said the same. In fact, to a noticeable degree my original four objectives for the church had been realized. This came only through the gracious empowering of God and willing cooperation of the people.

For some months I had been receiving telephone calls from the First Baptist Church of Maury City to see if I would consider pastoring them. Finally, I agreed to go for a trial sermon. They called me as pastor.

It was evident the church had great potential. The church field extended miles in every direction and the majority of people, especially from the outlying county area, were unchurched. I spoke to the pulpit committee and deacons about the need for an aggressive visitation program and a building program to make room for new people. They indicated a willingness to do these things if I would come as their pastor.

Even though it was difficult for us to leave our beloved Macedonia Church, we assumed the pastorate of the Maury City church, August 21, 1958. Some months later I began to regret the move. The church balked at entering a building program. Weekly, we saw indications that many had little desire to reach the poorer rural people. Even though the church supported me well, it broke my heart to see that so many prominent members were satisfied with the status quo of things.

Fortunately there were other members who were hungry for the Word and a deeper commitment to Christ. Among these were several ladies and new deacons whom we ordained: H. E. Jordan, Jr., and Willie Bob Ball. The response from our large group of young people was especially gratifying. While a few of the adults even objected to their voting in the business meetings, they had a larger vision of ministry than many of their elders.

At all of our pastorates Louise and I informed our congregations that our family wanted no other Christmas gift from the church than to see their hearty response to the special foreign missions offering. "Let's give our best Christmas gift to Christ," we urged.

We were saddened when we learned Maury City's 1957 Christmas offering to foreign missions was only $81. When I requested a goal of $250 for the 1958 Christmas offering, several objected saying we would do well to get $100. (I shocked them when I declared Louise and I planned to give that much.)

Before Christmas I received an unexpected check for $250 from Dr. and Mrs. Joe Moody of Houston, Texas. "Use it for anything you need," he wrote. I had seen them only once since we graduated together from Dyersburg High School. Instead of using it for myself, I told the church I was transferring it all to our budget and designating a good portion of it to the foreign missions offering.

"Now, what are you going to do?" I challenged them. They thrilled my heart by bringing the Lottie Moon Christmas offering to $500.

I sent a copy of our church newsletter to the Moodys and thanked them for inspiring our church to give its largest foreign mission offering ever.

But "the rest of the story," as Paul Harvey would say, is even more dramatic. Twelve years later I received a letter from Dr. Moody saying he had sent his check to me because he was angry with the Foreign Mission Board at the time. Then he was shocked to learn how a big portion of it wound up in the Lottie Moon Foreign Missions Offering anyway!

"I learned my lesson: don't mess with Lottie! I've been faithful in giving to the Christmas offering since that time."

Joe has given his own personal testimony about this experience many times. And on November 30, 1975, the *Baptist Bulletin Service* published my account of it in an article entitled "A Gift That Backfired." Only eternity will reveal how much has been raised for missions as a result of what the Moodys and I did.

In 1959 I accepted the invitation of Central Baptist Church in Flint, Michigan, to preach in a revival. God blessed with a great revival, and I made many friends in the area. During visitations I became burdened for Fenton, a residential city of 40,000. Situated on a lovely lake, it was about 20 miles south of Flint. Central Baptist Church asked if I would come back the following year and hold mission services in Fenton under their sponsorship. I gladly agreed.

Before my family arrived in Fenton, the Central Baptist Church rented a house for us to have services in, and a young couple opened their home for us to stay in each night. The Home Mission Board of the Southern Baptist Convention furnished two young summer missionaries to help Louise and me take a religious survey of the community and to assist in our services. We had Vacation Bible School in daytime and revival services at night.

At first we concentrated on the poorer, unchurched people. But God began convicting me as we drove by the mansions on Lake Fenton. After much prayer, Louise and I started knocking on the doors of these wealthy families, introducing ourselves, and explaining what we were doing in Fenton. They questioned us carefully to be sure we were not from a cult. (Most of them knew little or nothing about Baptists.) Then, to our surprise, several of these families invited us to come in and talk with them.

One lady, a wife of a vice-president at General Motors, told me God must have sent me for she had just been considering suicide. She said she and her husband were millionaires, but their souls were empty and lost. She received Christ when I witnessed to her and began attending our evening services in the little rented house.

We had similar experiences with some of the other wealthy families. Through these God impressed upon me that the "up and outs" may be reached as well as the "down and outs" if we take them his powerful gospel. I was reminded, as was Peter, that "God is no respecter of persons."[23] From this humble beginning, an active Southern Baptist church developed in Fenton.

At Maury City I encountered some racial and denominational prejudices. Some of my members were not happy when they learned I had become a friend of the black minister and sometimes visited in the homes of other blacks.

The Church of Christ had a larger attendance than did the Methodist or Baptist churches. Considerable jealousy and ill will sometimes existed between these groups. Behind my house I raised a big, productive garden. By sharing vegetables with the young Church of Christ minister, who lived on one side of my garden, I became better acquainted with him. In conversations, we found both of us liked to fish.

He accepted my invitation to go fish with me. We enjoyed the sport, but even more so the low-key religious conversations we had. We found that some of our differences were matters of terminology. In his library he had several of the same books I had in mine. I invited him to come visit me in my church office for further conversation and to see my other books. This he did.

Soon I heard that many members from both our churches objected to our fraternizing. Not long afterwards, he took another pastorate. I believe his church lost a good man.

Our little red-haired daughter Karis was born in June, 1959. Her name, adapted from the Greek word "charis," means gift or grace. And what a delightful gift to us she has proven to be! When I speak her name, I am often reminded of the favorite theme of my preaching: the grace of God.

Chapter 18
Racism, Reason, and Love

For the next five years I was pastor of the Calvary Baptist Church in Brownsville, Tennessee. This young church, located literally across the railroad tracks, was heavily in debt and had no pastorium. But it was an exciting and enthusiastic congregation, made up primarily of younger working families. I willingly took a cut in salary to undertake this work.

The previous year I had helped Dr. H. K. Sorrell in a revival at the Brownsville Baptist Church. There I became acquainted with many of the community leaders. Not long after I began working at Calvary, banker C. T. Hooper called me up about our great need for a pastorium.

"I know we do—badly, but we don't have the money," I said.

"Can you raise enough money to buy a lot for the home?" he inquired.

"Yes, but we would have nothing left for a down payment."

"One question: do you plan to stay with the Calvary Church for several years?"

"I certainly do," I replied.

"Well, the church has a poor credit rating right now with some outstanding bills. But I know your reputation for financial integrity. Our bank will lend Calvary the money for just a lien on the lot you secure."

"At five percent interest?" I ventured.

"You do drive a hard bargain," Mr. Hooper laughed. "We have only one loan out at present at five percent. But we'd like to help you and your people, so we'll make your loan for the same rate."

Immediately we went to work in earnest and soon bought a nice corner lot in a nearby subdivision. Knowing the needed arrangement for a pastor's home, Louise and I drew up a proposed floor plan. The church approved it with minor changes. Soon we had constructed a lovely brick pastorium. Then, in consultation with our treasurer, David Kail, we promptly arranged to pay off the church's operating debts. Increasingly we whittled away at our large building program indebtedness.

On December 16, 1961, Louise presented me with a little red-haired son, Joel. He is a namesake to the prophet Joel, who was both preacher and poet. Likewise our Joel is both a writer and earnest Bible student. We believe God has an exciting purpose for him.

I carried out a rather extensive counselling ministry, especially to families with marital problems. Judge Bernie Cobb sometimes referred couples to me. At times he had me come to his courtroom and talk with those in trouble. On occasions he even told couples seeking a divorce, "I will not proceed further with your divorce case until you have counselled with Bro. Kennedy."

Word spread through the community that I was willing to counsel with non-members as well as with members. And I charged nothing for my services. People sometimes came whom I had never seen before—alcoholics, drug addicts, individuals contemplating suicide, parents with wayward children, law violators battling a guilty conscience, persecuted Quakers, as well as the lost and backslidden. Sometimes when I was counselling with someone in my study, there would be five or six waiting to see me in the outside hallway or auditorium.

Occasionally a black family would send for me to come help them, and I would go. They were afraid to call in their own pastor lest he publicly expose their wrongs in his next church service. I always emphasized the need to get right with God before trying to cope with our personal problems.

When I returned home at night, it was not unusual to see a police car tailing me. I refused to be intimidated even though I had reason to believe the officers were members of the White Citizens Council. My purpose in the black community was spiritual, not political. Counselling, I discovered, is one of the most energy-depleting activities a minister can engage in.

I worked hard at personal visitation and sermon preparation. Louise and I sought to make our home a base of God's operation for the community. God blessed these efforts by us and our members, and we had many professions of faith and additions to the church.

Across the street from us a talented young professional couple moved named Raymond and Jan Saunders. They mowed their yard, cleaned their car, and did family washes on Sunday. We took the initiative in building a friendship with them, even though they were several years younger than we.

Soon the couple began making spiritual inquiry, and we led them to the Lord. Afterwards our church elected Raymond as our minister of music and Jan as our pianist. Our families have remained close friends over the years.

Later the Saunders moved to Sunbright, Tennessee. Raymond completed his doctor of theology degree and in 1971 founded the Caribbean College of the Bible, of which he is still president. It all began, not through a Sunday sermon or planned visitation, but through the loving example of a Christian home.

The *Baptist Bulletin Service* began purchasing little inspirational articles of mine (35 in all) and running them on the back of church bulletins. Each of these went to thousands of churches over the world and were read by over a million people. According to the editor of the *Baptist Bulletin Service*, "A man would have to preach to 450 people every Sunday for 50 years to speak to as many persons as the author of one bulletin article." Over the years that I contributed to this publication, I have met or heard from many people who have testified of being helped by some article. This outlet has also greatly enlarged the scope of my acquaintances.

Reprints of my church bulletin articles have appeared in many other publications. My first article, for instance, was picked up by the Fort Worth Tribune All-Church

Press. Someone sent me a copy of the newspaper of the St. Andrews Episcopal Church in that city with this written notation: "Congratulation on this fine article-and on making the front page." I have had letters from readers as far away as Hawaii.

I took a group of laymen and began services at the local County Home (a penal institution). Usually there are more black than white inmates. This ministry, begun so many years ago, is still going strong, thanks to dedicated laymen such as Robert Barden. Today Robert told me there have been 916 professions of faith in these services.

Since about half the population of Haywood County was black, racial tensions in those days mounted. Jobs, except for the most menial ones, generally were closed to blacks. For $2.00 to $3.00 per day it was easy to get a black woman to come and do the house cleaning, cooking, and babysitting for white families. When blacks tried to register to vote, they had to stand in line under the hot sun. When they did make it to the inside of the court-house, most were disqualified through various pretexts.

The most vocal protests came not from local blacks, who had born injustices so long, but from civil rights workers and groups who came to help and encourage. The local whites disdainfully labeled these people as "nigger lovers" and "outside agitators." At times they were able to gather a group of blacks onto the steps or lawn of the courthouse. But then police dogs were turned loose among them or a fireman hosed them with high-pressure water.

I pled for restraint and spoke out against violence and hatred. Some of the Christian people of my church and community agreed with me, but others were infuriated.

One of the big fears was that Negroes might attempt to attend our white churches. I pointed out that in Isaiah 56 God said even eunuchs, sons of the stranger, and outcasts of Israel should be welcomed to his house, "for mine house shall be called an house of prayer for all people."[24]

Also, I never could understand why whites would stand by blacks in a line before a supermarket cash register but wouldn't think of sitting by them for awhile in church. I contended that instead of viewing the Negro as our greatest social problem, we should see him in our greatest missionary opportunity. I knew it was hypocrisy to send our missionaries to live among the blacks of Africa when we tried daily to segregate ourselves from them in our own community.

Strong pressures were put on some of my deacons by their employers or community leaders to get me "to shut up and never again mention the Negro" from my pulpit. But when such motions were brought before the church, they would fail by a few votes.

As difficult as it was to depart from long-held tradition, an increasing number of Calvary Church members tried. The Womens Missionary Union sometimes collected and delivered clothes to needy black children. These dear members realized that I was just trying to apply the whole gospel to the whole person.

The Rev. Willie Grant Lyons, a black minister at Maury City, was earning a salary of $28 a month pastoring Mt. Pleasant Baptist Church. Additionally, he picked up about $4 a day doing odd jobs. He and his wife Robbie Mai had four children, ages 3-15. Then on November 1, 1964, Robbie Mai unexpectedly gave birth to quadruplets.

In my Sunday sermon I mentioned the plight of the Lyons family, whom I knew personally. Our congregation responded with an offering at the close of the service. But a more remarkable response came from a poor young couple who had been members of Calvary only a short time. They later handed me a plain envelope containing their wedding rings and one class ring.

"Sell these rings and give the money to the Lyons," they directed me. Also they charged that their names were not to be revealed.

While the names remained confidential, word of the generous act spread. A reporter from The Commercial Appeal of Memphis came and interviewed me about our church's dramatic response. It was published in the news-

137

paper on November 10 and doubtless helped publicize the needs and worthiness of the Lyons family. By a year later they had received some $13,000 and a new home was built for them.

My stance on Christian race relations did not go unnoticed by more progressive citizens of our community. I was elected a trustee of the Brownsville-Haywood County Library and helped to make it the first integrated public institution in our community. In 1965 I was elected chairman of the library board for the coming year. I reasoned with our police commissioner about the advantages of adding some black policemen to the force. A few months later he hired two: George Lewis Delk and Robert Lewis Wiley.

Upon hearing a report that my church was about to fire me, one prominent Jewish lady visited me and offered to come to Calvary Church with a group of Jewish friends to show their support and respect for me.

"Thank you, so much for your kind offer" I said, "but please don't, for that would get me fired even quicker."

Our church newsletter was sent to scores of people in our Community besides our members. One who received it was my good friend Morton Felsenthal, leader of the local Jewish synagogue. In a letter dated June 20, 1963, he warmly thanked me for including him on the circulation list of "The Calvary Caller." In his second paragraph he stated, "Your pastoral letter I have read and re-read and to my mind it brought forth the teachings of Jesus for all mankind to follow and emulate." Once he told me he would consider becoming a Christian if Christians actually followed the teachings and example of Jesus.

While pastor at Calvary I began driving to Memphis one or two days a week taking classes at Memphis State University. In May of 1965 the University awarded me the master of arts degree in English.

When I began taking the classes, I little realized that I would actually complete a degree. But God from the beginning purposed I should do so. About two months before I finished, Dr. J. K. Powell, vice-president of Campbellsville College, a Baptist senior college in Campbellsville, Kentucky, telephoned me.

"We need a good English instructor for the coming school year. Dr. Warren F. Jones, a former president of our college, has recommended you. Would you please come up here for an interview and look us over?"

Before agreeing, I asked, "Is the school racially integrated? I will not come if it isn't."

"Oh yes," he replied. "As a matter of fact we have students from a number of countries of the world."

Perhaps, I thought, this might become my mission field.

My daughter, Karis Moore, daughter-in-law, Julie Kennedy, and sons, Mark and Joel.

Our home at 400 N. Columbia in Campbellsville.

One of the "great little churches" I pastored.

Chapter 19

A New Career at Age 42

So I joined the faculty of Campbellsville College in September of 1965. I had to pinch myself to believe it was real, to realize that just before by 42nd birthday I was beginning a new career in higher education. This was a long way indeed from the cotton fields of my youth! I knew the Lord had an exciting purpose in it, and I was glad.

"Why do you want to come aboard a sinking ship?" asked Dr. La Rue Cocanougher as he interviewed me. He was the academic dean and was frankly pessimistic about the College's future.

"I can only say it was because the Lord brought me here," I replied. "When He is finished, He will have something else for me to do." The dean's pessimism did not alarm me. As a pastor I had grown accustomed to living with uncertainties. Yet the Lord had never failed me and my family. I knew he would continue being true to his promise, "I will never leave thee, nor forsake thee."[25]

More than 175 students enrolled in my classes some semesters. Then I was appointed faculty adviser to both the college newspaper and yearbook. I wanted to do my part, but soon I learned that I had been assigned more than my share of the responsibilities.

Some months later Dr. H. B. Evans, chairman of the English Department at Memphis State University wrote me a kind letter of congratulations on my new position. In it he shared a word of timely concern that I took to heart: "You have a total which constitutes a sinking weight. Be careful, therefore, that you do not break yourself down."

One of the courses I taught was Creative Writing. As an inspiration to my students I wrote along with them, sharing my own successes and failures. The fact that I was a published author also gave more credibility to my course.

On March 6, 1971, *Home Life* published my "The New Morality of our Sexy Sixties." It was run as the lead article and given a prominent four-page color spread. It emphasized that it was a sick society which "does not know the difference between proper sex and sex perversion, between normal sex interest and twisted sex obsession."

Over the years, more than 200 of my articles, sermons, poems, and book reviews have been published in more than 40 periodicals. These include such diverse publications as *Mature Living, The Deacon, Christianity Today, Grit, The Gideon, The Alliance Witness, Proclaim, Conquest, Good News Broadcaster, KPA bulletin, Christian Poetry Journal,* and *Lighted Pathway.* So my writing endeavour has been a ministry in itself and, hopefully, will continue speaking after I am gone.

After two years as instructor, I was asked to take chairmanship of the Department of Literature, Languages, and Library Science. Probably the largest of the College's eight departments, it also included the courses in speech, drama, and journalism. As a condition of my taking on this big responsibility, I asked that I be promoted to assistant professor and relieved of oversight of the college yearbook. Dr. Powell agreed. In 1969 I was promoted to associate professor.

Over the years I helped develop dozens of new courses as well as minors in journalism, drama, and library science. In 1973 I edited for the College a three-volume *Self-Study Report* required by the Southern Association of Colleges for us to gain full reaccreditation.

In 1974 I was selected as one of the evaluators of curriculum material for the Public Education Religion Studies Center of Wright State University, Dayton, Ohio. Over the years I participated in conferences and workshops of educators from over the United States. A large syllabus I compiled on teaching the Bible as literature received international circulation. Dr. John C. Howells, director of The Council for Christian Education in Schools, Melbourne, Australia, even wrote me for materials and assistance. I directed numerous conferences and work-shops at Campbellsville College, bringing to them nation-ally-know experts in their field.

As a member of the academic council, I worked with colleagues in clarifying the purposes of Christian educa-tion and improving the total curricula of the College. One of the most insightful papers I ever wrote, "The Real Test of Christian Education," was published as the lead article in *The Baptist Program* in February, 1985. Several other of my scholarly articles were published in such periodicals as *The Southern Baptist Educator*. My article in that publica-tion entitled "Freedom of the Press on a Christian Campus" received much commendation.

At the beginning of my courses I would usually address my students something like this:

"As you can detect from the syllabus of this course, I want to do for my students some things that a non-Christian professor cannot. Our various college disciplines are merely functional. But they must not be considered ends in them-selves, for the mastery of one or all disciplines is no guaran-tee that you will have success in life. This is because *life* is not English, science, music, or math. These disciplines right-ly related and employed may enrich our lives, however.

"As a Christian professor, I will put my courses in a dif-ferent frame of reference than would the non-Christian. My frame of reference will not be fragmented but more comprehensive and unified. I will try to help you see that all things are related in some way to everything else. You have not learned English rightly until you see its relation-ship to other disciplines of life—such as speech, history, religion, music, business, and science.

"As a Christian professor, I will view my subject from a different point of view than would the non-Christian. English, from a Christian point of view, can be interesting, exciting, and exceedingly profitable.

"As a Christian professor, I hope I will furnish an exam-ple in my own speech, life, and being that is of a higher quality than would the non-Christian.

"A truly educated person must have (1) knowledge, (2) skills, (3) standards and values. I will approach this course from all three of these important areas. It is in the third category of education that I have a distinct advantage over the non-Christian professor."

Finally, I challenged my students to study for the glory of God. I told them that God has a plan, a place, and a purpose for every life.

I have been astonished at the broad recognition I have received, most of it undeserved, of course. My biographical sketch has appeared in *Outstanding Educators of America, 1972; Directory of American Scholars, 1974; Contemporary Authors, 1974; Dictionary of International Biography, 1976-1977; International Who's Who in Community Service, 1976; Who's Who in the South and Southwest, 1977-78; Who's Who in Religion, 1977-78; Men of Achievement, 1978; Contemporary Journalists, 1978; Community Leaders and Noteworthy Americans, 1979-80;* and *The Directory of Distinguished Americans, 1981.*

Truly, God has given me an exciting and varied ministry as pastor, evangelist, college professor, missionary, and writer. Yet in all of these undertakings, the message has been Christian in nature. (One former student laughingly remarked, "You're the only professor I ever knew who preached literature.")

Many of our students came from underprivileged families and economically depressed areas. Because of my own humble background, I had no difficulty relating to them.

Our administration encouraged us faculty members to do additional graduate work, especially during summers. Consequently, I took a number of courses in literature and linguistics at the University of Kentucky and Eastern University.

An increasing number of foreign students began enrolling at our college. Some of them came upon the recommendation of missionaries. Others came because a counselor had told them they would get more individual attention at a small Christian school. Unfortunately, many of these students spoke and wrote very little English.

Dr. David Jester, our academic dean, asked me to develop and teach some English courses for international students. He knew that I related well to foreigners and had more graduate linguistic training than did any of the other English professors. However, my able colleagues did work with me in this program.

Undertaking this assignment was both an academic and spiritual challenge to me. Since I did not speak the languages of most of my students, I had to develop signs and symbols to illustrate my English words and phrases. But the students were highly motivated and made fast progress.

Some of the nationalities to whom I taught English were Venezuelans, Peruvians, Japanese, South African, Nigerian, Iranian, Jordanians, and Palestinian Arabs. Louise and I opened our home as well as our hearts to them. We became close friends with them and were able to share the gospel of Christ with them.

In 1968, Southwestern Baptist Theological Seminary offered me the opportunity to update my bachelor of divinity to a master of divinity degree. I was assigned 33 books to read from 11 fields of divinity studies. Also I was directed to review the texts and class notes from my B.D. program years previously.

Because of some unusual circumstances, I had only three weeks in which to read (or scan!) these books. Fortunately I am a fast reader.

Then I drove to Fort Worth and took an all-day examination. There were 550 objective questions, 50 from each of the 11 departments of study! When I finished, I probably was nearer to an emotional breakdown than I have ever been in my life. I wanted to scream! And I wanted to get away from Fort Worth, so I drove all the way to Little Rock, Arkansas, before stopping for the night.

You can imagine how elated I was when a few weeks later I received a congratulatory letter from Dr. Jesse Northcutt, dean of the school of theology. In part, it read:

"This is to notify you that you have passed the Master of Divinity comprehensive examination. Congratulations!

"It is not possible to reveal exact scores on this test. However, you will be interested to know that you ranked second among those who took the test (19). The score is designated as Superior ...."

Now having masters degrees in two fields made it easier for me to develop a Bible as Literature course and related workshops. It helped me to augment my new Church Public Relations course, which afforded credit for either journalism or religious education.

Beyond question, the Bible has exerted one of the strongest formative influences on Western literature. The renown literary critic Northrop Frye calls the Bible "the major informing influence on literary symbolism."[26] So without a fair knowledge of the Bible, the teacher of English and American literature is at a great disadvantage and often misinterprets.

Our campus newspaper, *The College Echo* (later renamed *The Campus Tymes*), served as a workshop for our journalism students. There was much unrest among college students of the late '60s and early '70s, so the task of a faculty adviser was sometimes a delicate one. My philosophy was that a campus newspaper should set the tone and spirit of a school but also exert a powerful force in making campus democracy work. I saw my role as that of a responsible and knowledgeable adviser rather than that of a censor.

Sometimes the administration felt that I allowed my staff too much liberty. Sometimes students felt that I exercised too much control.

But what I promoted was a free press within the bounds of Christian responsibility. To learn and mature, students had to be given liberty to experiment and even make mistakes. But they had no justification for being untruthful, unfair, or malicious.

One of our presidents (not Dr. Davenport!) censored and confiscated copies of a Christmas issue because it had a front page picture of two students kissing under some mistletoe. Evidently he thought it would give a bad image to the College if the public knew our students sometimes kissed.

I knew it gave a false image if we tried to persuade the public our students never kissed. So, with great concern, I promptly went to this president and told him to replace me as adviser if he was going to censor any more issues. He backed down.

Dr. W. R. Davenport was a gracious president who did not wish to be a censor. Many times he was embarrassed by something that appeared in the paper or disappointed when the tone seemed too negative, but he was always reasonable and approachable. Without his confidence in me and forbearance with immature students, our paper would have had great difficulty succeeding. My staffs respected and appreciated him.

For objective evaluation of our work, *The College Echo* secured membership in the Associated Collegiate Press, an All-American newspaper critical service. The first year of our membership, we were awarded a "Second Class" honor rating. The next year we received a "First Class" rating. Finally, in the spring of 1980 our paper, now *The Campus Tymes*, was awarded the coveted "All-American" rating, which included four of five possible marks of distinction. Again, in the spring of 1981, *The Campus Tymes* won the "All-American" rating with marks of distinction in all of the five possible categories.

"The 'All-American' rating is intended to be the highest honor a publication can receive," according to a release from the ACP. We were elated! Even though we operated on a shoestring budget with practically no lab equipment, we were putting out one of the finest small-college newspapers in the country. For a long time I had told my journalism classes we would some day attain "All-American." They believed it and dedicated themselves to what many would have considered an impossible task. But "all things are possible with God."[27]

As our school paper began gaining national recognition, the Associated Collegiate Press selected me as one of their judges, an honor of which I had never dreamed. Some of the papers I evaluated were from wealthy private schools and large universities.

But to me the most gratifying accomplishments were from my former journalism students who were becoming successful editors, columnists, and reporters for newspapers, newsletters, and magazines. They became a credit to our college that had given them opportunities to practice responsible journalism.

My journalistic skills were given wider outlets. In 1981, C. R. Daley, editor of the *Western Recorder*, state paper for Kentucky Baptists, decided to launch a statewide network of news correspondents to effect an enhanced coverage of local news, features, events, people, churches, and associations. He selected me as one of the nine stringers. I was assigned a fairly large area in Central Kentucky. During the next three years many of my news and feature stories were published, illustrated by my own photography.

Nothing was dull about teaching at Campbellsville College, except grading the papers sometimes. New texts and new courses helped keep my mind alert. In my 22 years on the faculty, I taught 33 different courses. Dr. James C. Hefley, one of the most prolific of Southern Baptist authors, holds a Ph. D. in communications from the University of Tennessee. On a visit with me in 1976, he said he believed I had the first Mass Communications Course in any Southern Baptist school.

I always contended that even though our college was small, we should be on the cutting edge of academic excellence. Change comes more slowly in the staid old colleges and universities.

During the years I served as chairman of our department, I was assisted and encouraged by a loyal and competent group of colleagues to whom I shall always be indebted. Though diverse personalities, we could usually reach an appropriate consensus.

Dr. Shirley Meece, whose specialty was literature and drama, was inquisitive, imaginative, and creative. Her brilliant mind was always searching for a better way to do everything. Mr. L. M. Hamilton had a love and compassion for his students that was unsurpassed. Mrs. Frances Roberts opened the hearts of her students to poetry and American Literature. Dr. Robert R. Doty brought a scholarly flair and a touch of England to all his courses. Mrs. Ruby Curry cheerfully accepted any assignment in composition or literature. Foster Eldredge, Donna Pirouz, and Eladio Bolanos guided their students through German, French, and Spanish. Librarians Brantley Parsley and Karen Lynema were excellent in library science.

Teaching at Campbellsville College made it possible for me to give my family members a college education, for members of faculty-families did not have to pay tuition. Also, I was privileged to have in some of my classes my wife, three of my children, my sister, and my wife's niece Elaine Newman who lived with us.

In May, 1987, after 22 exciting years on the faculty, I took early retirement. A few months later the College's board of trustees graciously granted me the official title of associate professor emeritus.

I'm grateful that I had the thrilling privilege of seeing God take the faculty, students, and curriculum of a small, struggling college and produce through it excellence in academics and life. I was a small part of a "treasure in earthen vessels."

Marching in 1984 graduation at Campbellsville College.

1987 Retirement Recognition at Campbellsville College.
President W.R. Davenport; English professors, L.D. Kennedy, Frances Roberts, L.M. Hamilton.

Treasure In Earthen Vessels

Chapter 20

More Than a Professor

"Professors aren't allowed to pastor churches," Dr. Powell informed me when I was employed by Campbellsville College. "The board of trustees has a policy against moonlighting."

Fortunately, from my first week in Campbellsville I began receiving calls to do supply preaching. My records reveal that I preached in 95 different Kentucky churches, some of them several times. I led Bible studies, discipleship workshops, missionary programs, and revival meetings (especially in the summers).

I was one of the first Kentuckians to be certified as a facilitator in our denomination's discipleship program known as MasterLife. For years I facilitated in state, associational, and church workshops. As a consequence, my horizons were enlarged and life enriched by the thousands of dedicated and interesting people whom I got to know.

During my ministry I have conducted 147 revivals in 12 states plus Brazil. Some were in large metropolitan churches, but most were in rural and small-town churches. One was a city-wide tent revival at Sturgis, Kentucky. In several instances, I have gone back two or three times to a given church. In 1966 I preached in ten revivals, including one in Mississippi and one in Tennessee.

All of this has been remarkable to me since I know I am not a conventional evangelist. In my preaching I have refused to water down the terms of the gospel in order "to get results." I have cautioned that saving faith is not just mental assent to sound doctrinal facts. Rather, it is a heart trust and surrender to Jesus Christ as our Saviour and Lord.

So I have not only emphasized grace, but also the necessity of repentance, that missing note of modern revivalism. Repentance is turning away from our rebellion and self-sufficiency and casting ourselves on Christ as God's all-sufficiency.

My invitations have been conducted differently from those of most evangelists. I have never tried to use psychological tricks, pressure, or scare tactics to get hearers to come forward and make a profession of faith. As I read somewhere when I was a boy, "A man convinced against his will is of the same opinion still." My formal invitations have not been lengthy unless people were responding.

Nevertheless, I have had the joy of witnessing some spirit-wrought revivals in which congregations were unified, backsliders reclaimed, broken lives and homes mended.

I have seen murderers, drunkards, ex-convicts, delinquent youths, immoral men and women, and self-righteous people converted. I have seen them come to Christ from all walks of life: college professors, students, bankers, business and factory workers, farmers, illiterates, and housewives. That is because salvation and revival are works of the Lord and not of the church or evangelist.

Twice I preached at a maximum security women's prison in Florida. These outcasts of society were lonely, bitter, discouraged failures. Some felt hopeless. Preaching once from Luke 8:41-48, I emphasized to the prisoners that the touch of one desperate, diseased, unknown woman in a shoving crowd halted the Lord of glory. I told them that Jesus was just as interested in them and their needs and was willing and able to change their lives and save them if they would repent and come to him by faith.

Their rapt attention and tearful responses when I gave the invitation reminded me that whoever comes to Christ, He "will in no wise cast out."[28]

In 1979 I was conducting services at the Salem Baptist Church near Campbellsville, Kentucky. At the close of the sermon an elderly farm woman, Carrie L. Warf, handed me a little poem she wrote during the service. At least the title fit me!

Non-Conforming Evangelist

The people were late;
The singing was slow;
I was just getting set
A-napping to go—
When the preacher knelt down to pray!

Forgetting to bow,
I stared at the man:
whenever, I wondered,
Since dawning began,
Did a pray-er *kneel down* to pray!

Sequestered they talked,
The man and his Lord—
There was reverent awe
In posture and word,
As he knelt (in a crowd!) to pray.

Then bowing, my heart
In humbleness made
A plea for such "mergence"
As that one displayed,
Kneeling, hidden in God, to pray!

— Carrie L. Warf

One never knows just what may happen in a revival service. One night in 1967, I was assisting pastor Nick Harris of the Latham's Chapel Baptist Church near Medina, Tennessee. The house was practically filled with people. The two suspicious-looking men who came in late had to walk all the way to the front to find a seat. It became evident that one of them was fairly intoxicated. I had hardly more than begun my sermon when he cried out, "Let'er rip, preacher!" Some of us had difficulty maintaining a straight face while two deacons ushered him out.

Ed and Eleanor Jones sold their fishing boat and bought a hardware store in the little resort town of Rockaway, Oregon. Upon their recommendation, the Rockaway Community Church asked me to come preach for a week. I tried to get out of the engagement since I was Southern Baptist and had no experience with a Community Church.

"If I came, I would have to preach the Bible as I understand it," I wrote the pastor. "It might cause some disturbance in your church."

"You will have full freedom in your preaching," he responded. "The Joneses have told us what kind of preacher you are, and we want to hear you. We've never had a revival in this church, and I believe we need one."

I agreed to come and preach the Word but told the pastor he would have to give his own invitations for church membership. He agreed.

What a glorious and unexpected week it proved to be! So many in the services were as hungry for the Word as were Ed and Eleanor when they had come to me years before. I had liberty in preaching, and the power of the Spirit filled the services with conviction and joy.

After each service a different family would invite me to their home. A large number of others from the church would accompany me to ask questions about the Bible and my beliefs. I sought to share them objectively and lovingly. We sometimes talked for hours.

A few months after my return home, I received in the mail a large letter in a manila envelope. The return address was that of the pastor in Rockaway. My heart sank, fearing he had written me a long letter about trouble that had developed for him as a result of my services.

Instead he thanked me for my help to them. He told me they had reorganized as the Rockaway Community Baptist Church and had adopted the New Hampshire Confession of Faith, a copy of which he enclosed. He said that members in regular standing were now required to be immersed.

In 1978 I held a revival one month in a Kentucky church and the next month in a church that had just split off from it and begun a new work. The pastors of both congregations were good men and former students of mine. We talked and prayed together. Then we firmly decided the split was misfortunate for both congregations. Each pastor graciously offered to resign and let the other one pastor both congregations if they would resolve their differences and reunite.

People from both congregations began attending the second revival. I preached on forgiveness, love, and going the second mile. People resumed speaking to one another again and shaking hands. Soon afterwards the two congregations were reunited in the original church. To me that was revival!

Missionaries Donald and Betty Spiegel invited me to come to Teresina, Brazil, then a city of 350,000 near the Equator. So in the summer of 1980 I went to help them in evangelism and missions for about 19 days. I went there to minister, not sightsee!

Soon after my arrival, I preaching at Alvarada. Under the leadership of missionary Peggy Pemble, this church had been organized for only a few months.

My first words to the congregation, in faltering Portuguese were, "My friends, I do not speak Portuguese." With that I went back to English sentences and let Don interpret in their native language. Speaking Portuguese better than most of them, he beautifully translated both my thoughts and emotions.

During the next few nights I preached at Redonda, a mission on the outskirts of Teresina, started by the Spiegels in 1979. Present the first night were 95, the largest attendance in the history of the mission. One man, about 35, made a profession of faith as I concluded a simple message on John 3:16.

Don remarked that the simple little building at Redonda had been constructed of "discarded bits and pieces." I supposed that one might say the same of the lowly people who worshipped there. It reminded me that throughout history Christ has been doing the same—taking broken hearts and mending them, taking broken lives and transforming them into something useful.

Nowhere have I ministered to any people more friendly, kind, and gracious than the Brazilians. Some hugged me the first time they met me. Even the little children gathered around me and tried to talk with me.

Braz and Maria De Costa gratefully moved from their mud-thatched hut into a house that God had provided. With about 50 neighbors and Christian friends present, I brought a dedication message for their new home. The sincere rejoicing of the fellow Christians over the good fortune of the De Costas was thrilling. There seemed to be no jealousy whatsoever.

One Wednesday night I led a service at beautiful Catarina Church. There I met an ex-prostitute who had been converted listening to Dr. Nilson Fanini (called the Billy Graham of Brazil).

She first wrote Fanini for a Bible, told him she was a prostitute, and signed her letter, "One with a lonely heart." After continuing to listen to his broadcasts and receiving correspondence from him, she accepted Christ and quit her business. She signed her last letter to him, "One whose heart is no longer lonely." With radiant face, she told me that she then was truly happy.

Don Spiegel also served as director of the 12-acre Piaui State Baptist Campground, some miles from Teresina. We made several trips out there in daytime. Once we loaded rocks from a rock pile into his Volkswagon and filled in deep holes in the entrance road. On each trip we hauled several barrels of lime to be used in building an addition to the dining hall.

Once when we got stuck in the mud, I jumped out and helped two Brazilian workers push. From comments they made about this and other work I did, I found that by my actions I was actually preaching all the time. They said I must be a Christian for even though I was an

American college professor, I did not seem to feel I was better than they.

Jacinta, the Spiegel's 21-year-old kitchen maid spoke no English. She was a neat, superb cook, and quite intelligent. She hoped to complete high school at night and then be admitted to university studies.

Jacinta got up about 5:00 a.m. and caught a bus to the Spiegels at 5:30. By 7:00 she had breakfast on the table. Then after washing dishes, she started lunch, which was served at 11:30. During the afternoons she often washed and ironed clothes before preparing supper. The Spiegels gave her a bus token at 6:30 p.m., and she proceeded to night school, returning to her home about 11:00 p.m. In spite of that hard life, she smiled and sang a lot.

My heart went out to Jacinta, so I smiled at her and complimented her cooking. I tried out my new Portuguese phrases and sentences on her. That seemed to please her.

One day I was sitting in the living room preparing a sermon. Presently I became conscious that Jacinta was standing quietly by my side, waiting for my attention. Then she handed me a piece of paper that I supposed I had dropped in the kitchen. But when I opened it, I saw she had printed in large letters in English:

I LIKE YOU.

YOU LIKE ME.

☐ YES

☐ NO

I checked the "yes" and wrote before it "muito" (very). She beamed proudly and walked softly back to the kitchen.

Even though Jacinta was a Catholic and short of spare time, she came to the service at Alvarada Baptist Church at which I administered the ordinances. While I spoke my uncertain Portuguese before baptizing each convert, she smiled reassuredly. I realized she was another lonely soul, overlooked my most people but important to God. She responded to the language of love and acceptance.

While in Brazil, I spoke at several other churches and missions. One of the highlights of my trip was preaching one starlit night at an open-air service far out in the bush country. With the dazzling Southern Cross above and a yardful of eager Brazilians around me, I proclaimed again the "wonderful story of love."

After my message four women and two men came forward to receive Christ. One of the women, very old, hugged me firmly in appreciation.

Before leaving Campbellsville I was warned about barber flies that are present in Equatorial Brazil. They are carriers of an incurable disease that causes heart muscles to degenerate. They are pretty large and come out at night when lights are out.

But I knew a worse disease—SIN—was causing millions of poor Brazilians to eternally perish. So I committed myself into the Lord's hands and did not worry about the barber flies. I knew that the believer who tries to play it safe and save himself will never do much for others.

The last Sunday I preached at Redonda they observed "The Day of the Pastor," an annual occurrence in Brazilian churches. Don and I were invited to special seats at the front to be honored. They presented Don with a roll of electrical tape that he so often needed to repair one of his cars on the road.

They had watched me taking notes in a small spiral notebook, which I kept in my shirt pocket. So they gave me a souvenir notebook of Brazil.

As the laymen presented the gift to me, he made a touching speech about how I had demonstrated to them the true meaning of love and had given them a better understanding of the Great Commission.

He spoke about how humbled they were that I, an American professor, had actually come into their little mud huts to get to know all the members of their families.

I was deeply moved by the kindness and appreciation of these gracious people. I'm sure I learned more from them than they did from me.

What I did during my mini-missionary stint was nothing compared to the work of the career missionaries. With affection and amazement, the Brazilians called Don Spiegel a "man of seven instruments." In their idiom that means a man who can do anything.

For instance, he sang, taught, counselled, and preached regularly. But he also welded; repaired his automobile and washing machine; did carpentry, plumbing, electrical work, blockmaking, and blocklaying; painted portraits and landscapes; operated a ham radio; repaired furniture and electronic equipment; cut his own hair; half-soled shoes; and served as an architect and contractor for church and mission buildings.

Impressed upon me by my brief experiences was the fullness of missionaries' lives and the variety of things they do to demonstrate and share the love of Christ with those around them. I have become more conscious that all believers are on mission for Christ, whether we head for the field, the factory, the schoolroom, the doctor's office, our neighbor's house, or a vacation. If we will use the opportunity, there are so many ways to share Christ with others.

As my plane left Teresina, I looked down upon the poor women washing their children and clothes in the River Poty. It reminded me of how God wants to take our soiled and sinful lives and wash us "whiter than snow."

Arab girl I met at ruins of Old Jericho.
She spoke three languages!

Girl at Bethany washing clothes
much as I did when I was her age.

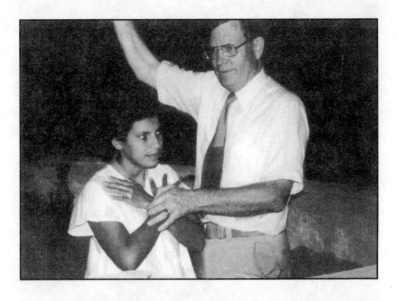

One of six L.D. baptized in outdoor baptistry, Teresina, Brazil.

Our men from Friendship Church did mission work with Baptist Builders.

Chapter 21

Great "Little" Churches

In the summer of 1969 I drove down a winding gravel rode to the Mt. Gilboa Baptist Church to help pastor Ken Adams in a revival. In this little church, 12 miles from Campbellsville, Kentucky, I saw many things that surprised and excited me.

Bro. Adams and Edwin Parrott disagreed openly on some interpretations with James Hunt, the teacher, during the Sunday School lesson. But they were cordial with one another after the service was over.

In the discipleship meeting, Lyla Parrott asked some unBaptistic questions but was not turned out of the church. I perceived that the members there loved and respected one another. They exemplified unity on essentials and charity in non-essentials. There was unity in a healthy diversity.

"If I ever pastor again," I told Ken, "I want it to be a church like Mt. Gilboa."

About two years after this the College relaxed its policy against "moonlighting" and began allowing us preachers to pastor small churches. Bro. Adams had resigned at Mt. Gilboa to go elsewhere.

On September 5, 1971, I accepted the call from Mt. Gilboa. For nearly 13 happy years I was their bivocational pastor. My tenure at the church was the longest of any of its pastors.

Outward appearances and pompous statistics were not what attracted me to Mt. Gilboa. With a $10,000 budget, the church had averaged 38 in Sunday School during the two years prior to my becoming their pastor. It was so far back "in the wildwood" that visitors often got lost going there. And when they arrived, they found a little wooden building with a metal roof. During the services, the music came from an old-fashioned pump organ. Yet I consider Mt. Gilboa one of the greatest churches I have ever known.

In many ways they reminded me of the church at Smyrna. To it Christ said, "I know your poverty—yet you are rich!"[29] Smyrna was poor in material things but rich toward God, rich in faith, rich in sacrifice and helpful works. Laodicia, on the other hand, was a poor rich church whose treasures were on earth. Smyrna was a rich poor church whose treasures were in heaven.

Was Mt. Gilboa a poor church? Don't judge by the size of its building, the number of its members, the amount of its budget, nor the salary of the pastor. Ask rather, how much did the members love one another? How loyal were pastor and people to the Lord?

Too long we have measured progress, success, and dedication in quantitative terms. But true spirituality cannot be measured statistically nor numerically. It is not in bigness nor busyness, but in faithfulness. Increased attendance and activity in our churches mean little unless conduct and lives of the members are being changed and made more Christlike.

Mt. Gilboa was a rich poor church, a great little church!

Before agreeing to become pastor, I inquired about the boundaries of their church field. They told me the field went only two miles from north to south and two from east to west. Fewer than 100 people lived on the field.

"If your church field extends no further than that, I cannot pastor you," I declared. "Jesus said, 'The field is the world.'[30] If you are willing to reach out in love to the world, I will accept your call. But I must warn you, if you do that, God will send your way many people who are different from those you have been accustomed to. Unless you sincerely welcome them and seek to minister to them, I will resign." They agreed to my terms.

The first test came when one of my black students, Elizabeth White, began attending our services. There were no blacks in our community, but they accepted Elizabeth. She won to the Lord her boyfriend Joe, a black disc jockey. Soon thereafter he answered God's call to preach and enrolled in Southern Baptist Theological Seminary.

Our people fell in love with Saba, a brilliant Ethiopian girl who began attending and taught one of our mission studies.

Two Japanese exchange students, Yukihiko Kitano and his friend Masashi, stayed in our home for several days. These young Buddhists accompanied us to services at Mt. Gilboa. A Gideon in our church presented each of them a Japanese/English Bible. They were so grateful and continued corresponding with us after returning to Japan.

Our family and church realized that one does not have to go himself to be a foreign missionary.

As word circulated that Mt. Gilboa lovingly welcomed all nationalities to its services, we had in attendance Palestinian Muslims, an Iranian, Peruvians, a Nicaraguan, Costa Ricans, Cambodians, Mexicans, and Venezuelan Catholics.

Ron Pillay, a brilliant black from Johannesburg, Soweto, South Africa, came in 1981 to the United States to study. Ron had a background of robbery and violence before experiencing the transforming power of Jesus Christ. Much of his youth had been spent in prisons for various crimes. Many whites in the States still feared him (as many believers feared Saul of Tarsus after his conversion).

Mt. Gilboa Church and I befriended Ron, welcomed, and discipled him. Eventually he received the bachelor of science, master of divinity, and doctor of ministry degrees. In 1987 he came back and visited with my family for four days.

Ron told me again how much Mt. Gilboa Church had meant to him because "the people accepted me." He wanted to go there once again, so I drove him out to the community. He went inside the church building and meditated. Then I took him to visit several families whom he specially loved. And Ron had made a difference in their lives.

Greg and Susie Jewell moved into the edge of our community. He was the assistant manager of the local McDonalds. Greg was Free Evangelical and Susie an independent Presbyterian. At first they were cool toward our visits, contending that Baptists were theologically liberal. But we continued to reach out to them in love.

After the birth of their first child Benji, Susie had to be hospitalized for some time. Louise and I brought Benji home with us, let him sleep between us and gave him formulas of goat's milk. When the Jewell's well went dry, Ed and Lyla Parrott invited them to their house to do their family washing. Other members helped them in various ways.

Unable to resist our friendship any longer, the Jewells began attending Mt. Gilboa Baptist Church. On the day they presented themselves for baptism, they announced God had called them to be foreign missionaries. Soon afterwards, we held a dedication service for them, and they moved to Fort Worth. After Greg completed his studies at Southwestern Baptist Theological Seminary, they were appointed Southern Baptist missionaries to Brazil.

Another young couple, just married, moved into an old dilapidated house in our community. They were Edward and Sharon Smith. We invited them to church. With his long hair and 12-string guitar and with her tight jeans and boots, the Smiths didn't look like everyone else at Mt. Gilboa. But our women took Sharon "under wing" and mothered her. Some of the men took a chain saw and cut firewood for Ed.

We found that Ed composed beautiful spiritual songs, accompanying himself on the piano, guitar, and harmonica. With one of the sweetest voices we had ever heard, Sharon sang like a mockingbird.

Mt. Gilboa discipled them and gave them opportunities to develop as musicians and counselors. After graduating from Campbellsville College, Ed completed masters and doctoral degrees at Southwestern Baptist Theological

Seminary and at Midwestern Baptist Theological Seminary.

Ed served a few years as the associate pastor and minister of education and singles in some metropolitan churches. Then the Smiths returned to Campbellsville, Kentucky. Ed established and operates a unique Family Care Counseling Center there. He and Sharon conduct marriage enrichment seminars and give musical concerts in many states.

These are just a few of the scores of people God sent to us for our love and ministry. The transformation and spiritual growth in their lives was sometimes almost unbelievable.

Mt. Gilboa beautifully exemplified a key quality of a spiritual church: unconditional acceptance of others (Romans 15:7).

The "little" church also excelled in giving. When I became their pastor, they were already giving ten percent of their meager receipts through the denomination's Cooperative Program (for world missions). This was steadily increased to 34 percent by 1983. *The Western Recorder* reported that in both 1981 and 1983 Mt. Gilboa was third among Kentucky churches in per capita giving through the Cooperative Program.

The church also gave thousands annually through local, home, and foreign mission offerings. William G. Tanner, Executive Director-Treasurer of the Home Mission Board of the Southern Baptist Convention wrote us in 1979:

> Because of your commitment to Home Missions and your generous spirit of stewardship, your congregation is one of the top ten churches in the Kentucky Baptist Convention in per capita resident member gifts to the 1978 Annie Armstrong Easter Offering.... You have set an example for every church in the state of Kentucky.

The congregation at Mt. Gilboa worshipped with dignity and fervor. The presence and power of God were awesome.

In many churches Sunday School has been labeled "the most wasted hour of the week." Not so at Mt. Gilboa. The church had an intensive teacher-training program, and the Bible was taught interestingly and with spiritual depth. We built an educational annex to improve our teaching environment.

Without the help of other members, there is no way I could have adequately pastored Mt. Gilboa and fulfilled my duties at Campbellsville College. They realized I was pastor and all the members were called to minister.

After a detailed study of the New Testament concept of deacon, we initiated a Deacon Family Ministry Plan that really worked. It was more than a visitation program, though visits were involved. It was a loving, caring relationship of the deacons and every member of every family in the church.

At the monthly deacons' meetings, they did not discuss church business in general. Rather they reported on needs and concerns of their assigned families that were discovered in their contacts during the previous month. They kept me informed of special needs and crises requiring my ministry.

Often when I arrived at the hospital or funeral home, I found waiting with the family the deacon who had been assigned to them.

Edgar Russell and Carl Hunt were two of the most compassionate deacons I have ever known. Darrell Hunt was a pastor's best friend and wise adviser. His counsel and suggestions were respected not only by our members but by people throughout our area. He was also an effective lay preacher. The other deacons likewise took their ministry seriously.

In 1983 *The Deacon* magazine published an article of mine about our Family Ministry Plan that was instrumental in helping some other churches set up a similar one.

Sensing that the church now needed and could support a full-time pastor, I resigned on December 31, 1983. Later the church kindly elected me pastor emeritus.

I'm glad that from my first visit to Mt. Gilboa Church, God gave me eyes to see there the "treasure in earthen vessels."

After retiring from Campbellsville College, I did not plan to pastor again. Revival, supply, and interim work kept me as busy as I wanted to be.

In 1988 I became interim pastor of the Friendship Baptist Church near Campbellsville. It was a historic old church whose actual date of organization was unknown. It is known that it was admitted into the fellowship of the Russell Creek Association in 1807 under the name of Sand Lick Meeting House. It is also known that Luther Rice preached in the church in 1815. He took what is believed to be the first offering for missions in Kentucky.

But I found that this old church, proud of its heritage, had been pretty much asleep for years. By God's power I tried to awaken them. I shamed them for sending their children to Sunday School classes in what I called the dungeon (a musty basement, some rooms of which had no windows). I told them how badly they needed a modern children's annex with appropriate furniture and bathrooms.

When I returned from two weeks of revivals in Tennessee, Friendship told me they had called me as pastor while I was away.

"I'm sorry!" I protested. "I told you I don't want to be pastor."

"But we voted by secret ballot and you received a unanimous call—something that has never happened at our church to our knowledge. We also voted to build the educational building, renovate our basement, and install a baptistry if you will be our pastor. We want to do those things but need your leadership."

When I was convinced of the sincerity of their promises, I agreed to lead them until we completed the building program and other additions. We elected short-range and long-range planning committees who studied the Biblical mission of our church, our ministry needs, and facility improvement needs.

A few months later, with $921 in our building fund and an average weekly attendance of 46 in Sunday School, we decided to go into what for us was a big building program. I designated April 30, 1989, as Building Program Day and asked them to bring $10,000 in cash and checks so we could begin work.

So sure were we that God would provide that we announced ahead of time a victory dinner to follow the fundraising morning service. What a step of faith for Friendship Church! But God honored it.

Our little band of about 50 gave an offering that morning of $10,720 plus $8,820 in pledges. We praised God, ate joyfully, and had a ground-breaking that very afternoon.

We applied to the Ervin G. Houchens Foundation for a $20,000 interest-free loan to be repaid within five years. The loan was approved and check received.

During the next few months thousands of dollars worth of volunteer work was contributed—concrete work, carpentry, electrical, plumbing, painting, insulation, and meal preparation for the work crew. Men, women, and young people worked side-by-side, giving cheerfully and sacrificially of their time and abilities. One of our members, Barry Blevins, was an experienced contractor. He served without pay as the chairman of the building committee, subcontractor, and overseer of the total project.

Before long we had completed what was probably the brightest and most modern children's annex in Taylor County. In facilities and improvement the church went far beyond the original plans.

The secret of our success lay in the faith, hope, and love of our members. The same might be said of them as was of the wallbuilders in Nehemiah's day: "the people worked with all their heart."[31]

The building and renovations were completed without our borrowing a penny of money at interest. In fewer than five years the interest-free loan from the Houchens Foundation was repaid.

Best of all, we could sense a surge of new life, joy, enthusiasm, and faith in our church. Attendance and offerings increased, souls were saved, and new members added. TO GOD BE THE GLORY!

On February 25, 1990, I performed the first baptisms inside our own building in Friendship Church's more than 183-year history. That also was my last Sunday as pastor. The care of the church was transferred into the capable hands of our young associate pastor, Fred Miller, Jr.

Paul heard the Macedonian call once. I heard it three times! We moved back to Ripley, Tennessee, on September 1, 1994. Macedonia Baptist Church called me as their interim pastor on September 7. At a later business meeting, when I was absent, the church voted to name me their pastor emeritus.

We regretfully expected to leave Macedonia when a new pastor arrived on the field. Since I had such a long-standing relationship with the church, I feared that my continuing presence might create problems or make him uncomfortable.

But Pastor Stephen Williams visited us, graciously requesting Louise and me not to leave. He said he had checked me out with other preachers and was confident I would help, not hinder, his ministry. He stressed that I could be a valuable resource to him through my knowledge of the church and its members.

So we are still enjoying fellowship at Macedonia. We love the dear people there, who are like family to us. We love Bro. Williams and seek to encourage and support him fully. His preaching and teaching are excellent. He frequently calls upon me to preach or assist him in a service.

Friendship and Macedonia churches are also great little churches where there is much "treasure in earthen vessels."

Some of the International students to whom I taught basic English; Iranian, Venezuelans, Palestinians.

Standing by Friendship Baptist Church with my associate, Fred Miller (now the pastor).

Conclusion

Besides Jesus Christ, the "pearl of great price," I found another treasure years ago. She was Louise Newman when I found her on a farm at Hurricane Hill near Ripley, Tennessee. She was and is outwardly beautiful. But I was more attracted by her inner beauty: Christian character, intelligence, unselfishness, and a sweet and gentle spirit that makes one comfortable in her presence. I wooed and won her as my wife.

Through the years Louise has been a faithful, loving helpmate and unpaid secretary. She cared for me and our children and others who lived with us from time to time. She was hospitable to lonely students, foreigners, friends, and church members. She sewed for the family, cooked great meals, canned, froze the food from our organic garden, and took myriad telephone messages for me. She assisted with my pastoral visitation and counselling. She and our dear children have been an invaluable encouragement to me in the writing of this book. My daughter Karis is typing the manuscript.

One of the things that Louise and I like about the rural pastorate is that here we can get so close to the lives and problems of our people. Ministering to others (even ones whom society passes over) is not a degrading activity. Did not Jesus say, "And whosoever of you will be chiefest, shall be servant of all."[32]

In your service for Christ, He may ask you to "take the lowest place."[33] If so, be cheerful and give of your best.

But He may say to you, "Friend, move up to a better place."[34] If so, go up humbly and never feel superior to those in lower places. You, too, are still an earthen vessel.

A reporter once asked me how I would like to be remembered. My reply went something like this:

"I don't care whether people remember what courses I taught at the College or the titles of sermons I preached in churches. Rather, I would like for them to remember me as a man who loved everybody. The children as well as the adults. The blacks as well as the whites. The simple people as well as the educated. The poor as well as the privileged. I hope God will be able to say, 'L. D. was faithful.'"

If these things should be so, then my life will have been truly successful.

Turkey Creek, Macedonia, and Poplar Springs churches
all celebrated my 50th Anniversary in ministry.

L.D. and Louise at Turkey Creek's celebration.

Pastor Stephen Williams presents me
a plaque from Macedonia Church.

Notes

INTRODUCTION

1. R. Lofton Hudson, *A Good Likeness in the Looking Glass—After 60* (Nashville: Convention Press, 1985), 124. Used by permission.
2. Proverbs 17:22 NIV.
3. James 2:1-7 NIV.
4. Isaiah 5 1:1 NIV.

Chapter 1.
FROM COTTON PATCH TO COLLEGE PROFESSOR

5. Mark 9:23 KJV.
6. Matthew 23:11 NIV.

Chapter 5.
WE GET A MODEL-T FORD!

7. Philippians 4:11 NIV.

Chapter 6.
THE DAY I'LL NEVER FORGET

8. Galatians 2:20 KJV.
9. Romans 3:23 KJV.
10. Romans 6:23 NIV.
11. 2 Corinthians 5:21 NIV.

Chapter 7.
TO BOGOTA AND THE BOOGER FARM

12. Mark 13:32 KJV.

Chapter 9.
THE 1937 FLOOD

13. Proverbs 13:7. From *The Holy Bible: The Berkley Version In Modern English* (Grand Rapids, MI: Zondervan Publishing House, 1959).

Chapter 10.
LIVING IN A SCHOOLHOUSE

14. Philemon 1:2 NIV.

Chapter 11.
DISCOVERING THE POWER OF WORDS
15. Proverbs 18:24 KJV.
16. Matthew 10:31 KJV.

Chapter 12.
FROM SHARECROPPER TO CHEMICAL
OPERATOR AT OAK RIDGE
17. Ezekiel 33:7-9 KJV.

Chapter 13.
"LET NO MAN DESPISE THY YOUTH"
18. 1 Timothy 4:12 KJV.
19. Ecclesiastes 7:16 NIV.

Chapter 14.
NEVER A DULL MOMENT
20. Matthew 10:36-37 KJV.
21. Mark 10:29-30 KJV.

Chapter 17.
A MISSION-CENTERED MINISTRY
22. L. D. Kennedy, "The Christian Policy Toward Other Races," *Home Missions*, May, 1955, 6.
23. Acts 10:34 KJV.

Chapter 18.
RACISM, REASON, AND LOVE
24. Isaiah 56:7 KJV.

Chapter 19.
A NEW CAREER AT AGE 42
25. Hebrews 13:5 KJV.
26. Northrup Frye, *Anatomy of Criticism: Four Essays* (Princeton University Press, 1957), 316.
27. Mark 10:27 NIV.

Chapter 20.
MORE THAN A PROFESSOR
28. John 6:37 KJV.

Chapter 21.
GREAT "LITTLE" CHURCHES

29. Revelation 2:8 NIV.
30. Matthew 13:38 NIV.
31. Nehemiah 4:6 NIV.

CONCLUSION

32. Mark 10:44 KJV.
33. Luke 14:10 NIV.
34. Luke 14:10 NIV.

- END -